W9-ANJ-703

GUITAR *signature licks*

Jimi HENDRIX

A Step-by-Step Breakdown of His Guitar Styles and Techniques

By Andy Aledort

Cover Photo: David Redfern / RETNA LTD.

ISBN 0-7935-3659-6

HAL•LEONARD®
CORPORATION

7777 W. BLUEMOUND RD. P.O. BOX 13819 MILWAUKEE, WI 53213

Visit Hal Leonard on the internet at http://www.halleonard.com

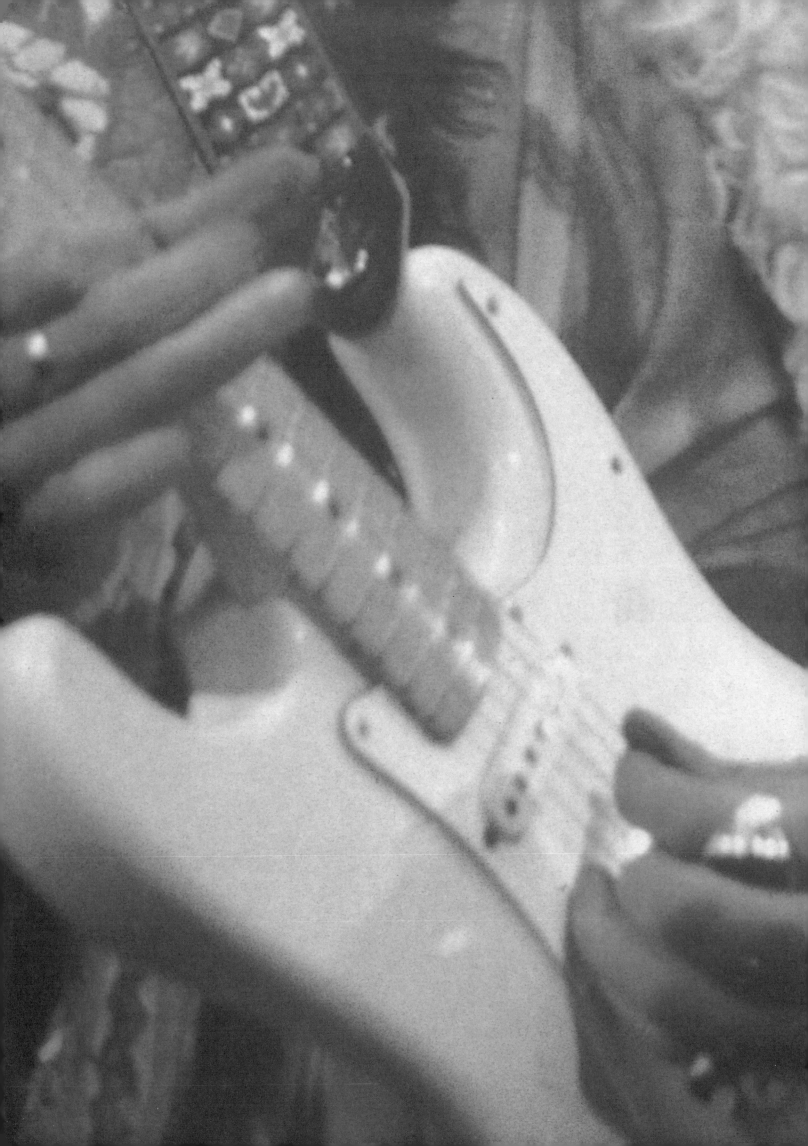

GUITAR *signature licks*

Jimi HENDRIX

INTRODUCTION

Jimi Hendrix—he's the guy that took a plain old Fender Stratocaster and turned it into a sonic surfboard, a ferocious assault weapon, an instrument of unparalleled beauty, a rocketship chartered on a journey beyond the unknown. With burning intensity and boundless creativity, Hendrix gathered a vast spectrum of guitar styles—blues, jazz, R&B, soul, and rock 'n' roll—and twisted them together to create a sound and style that was truly *revolutionary*. In rock guitar, there are but two eras—Before Hendrix and After Hendrix. When Jimi came along, he knocked the music world completely out of its orbit and forever rewrote the book on both guitar and contemporary music. He remains, without question, one of the most influential musicians that has ever lived.

Jimi Hendrix Signature Licks offers a unique and thorough examination of twelve of Hendrix's greatest compositions. Each song is segmented into individual sections such as intro, verse, chorus, bridge, solo, and outro. Each song segment is presented with all of the guitar parts fully transcribed, plus accompanying audio on CD, as performed by a full band. All solos, as well as complex rhythm parts, are also performed slowly for easier consumption and understanding. Performance notes, outlining chord voicings, scale use, unusual techniques, etc., are included in the text for each song. On the accompanying CD, the attempt was made to recreate the sound of the original recordings in terms of guitar tone and panning. In most cases, the rhythm guitar is panned to the right, and the lead guitar is panned to the left. Overall, the intent of this recording is to present a mix that accentuates the guitar more clearly than as it appears on the original recordings. This package—CD, written transcriptions, and performance notes—offers a complete picture of Jimi's playing on each of these classic songs. On the CD, each musical excerpt begins with a four-count ("One, two, three, four...") as sounded by the clicking together of drumsticks. The only exception is the solo section of "Hey Joe," which begins with a three-count click to be thought of as "Two, three, four..."

THE RECORDING

All of the musical tracks were recorded on a Tascam DA-88 digital eight-track recorder, combined with a Mackie 1604 sixteen-channel mixing board, mixed down to a Tascam DA-30 DAT machine. Signal processing included an Alesis Midiverb 4, Alesis Microverb III, Alesis 3630 compressor, and a Rane RE-14 stereo equalizer.

The guitar used exclusively on all tracks was a 1961 Fender Stratocaster with rosewood fretboard, fitted with Seymour Duncan SSL-1L pickups. Strings were D'Addario XL125s. The amplifier used on all tracks was a 1978 Marshall MK II 1959 master model 100-watt lead (tweaked by George Saer of GT Electronics—thanks, George) played through a 300-watt Marshall 1960 "A" 4x12 cabinet (previously owned by John Paul Jones of Led Zeppelin). Additional amplification was provided by a Bruno Underground 30. All guitar parts were recorded with Shure SM-58 and Beta-58 microphones. Distortion pedals were Dunlop Fuzz Faces (red and blue) and an original Roger Mayer Octavia, and the wah-wah was a reissue Vox.

Two basses were used—a 1962 Gibson EB-2 and a 1986 ESP J-Bass (fitted with Seymour Duncan "Bass Lines" pickups). The bass amplifier was a 1972 Fender Bassman 135 played through a 1988 Marshall JCM 800 "1551" 2x15 cabinet. Shure SM-57s were used to record the bass.

The drum tracks (played magnificently by Ed Cavaseno) were performed on a late '50s/early '60s Gretsch six-piece drum kit with Zildjian and Paiste cymbals and Tama drumsticks. A combination of Sennheiser MD 441 and AKG 451 & 452 EB microphones were run into a Tascam M-208 eight-channel mixing board, recorded direct to a Sony 75ES DAT machine. The DAT master of the drum tracks was then flown onto two tracks on the DA-88.

BIG, BIG THANKS TO: My family—Tracey, Rory, and Wyatt, and my mom; drum-meister Ed Cavaseno; Brad Tolinski, Dennis Page, Jimmy Brown, and everyone at Guitar World/Guitar School; Jeff Schroedl, John Cerullo, and everyone at Hal Leonard Corp.; Flip Van Domburg Scipio, Leroy Aiello, and everyone at Mandolin Brothers; Mitch Colby, Nick Bowcott, and everyone at Marshall/Korg; George Saer at GT Electronics; Tony Bruno at Bruno Custom Amplification.

SPECIAL THANKS TO: Jimmy Dunlop at Jim Dunlop USA; Don Dawson at D'Addario Strings; Davida Rochman at Shure Brothers; Brian Birmingham at Seymour Duncan Pickups; Steve Blucher at Dimarzio, Inc.; Bill Mohroff at TEAC, America; James Fowler at Mackie Designs, Inc.

This book is dedicated to my father.

SPANISH CASTLE MAGIC
Words and Music by Jimi Hendrix

Allegedly named after a music club that Jimi frequented in his hometown of Seattle—the Spanish Castle—this is one of a handful of tunes Jimi wrote in the key of C♯ minor. Jimi favored this key because it allowed him to take advantage of the giant minor third sounded by the open low E string. Other tunes in C♯ minor which make abundant use of the open low E are "Freedom" and "Long Hot Summer Night." The open high E and B strings also add ringing sustain to his C♯m7 chord voicing.

"Spanish Castle Music" features a twist on the Experience line-up: it's really three Jimis and a Mitch (Mitchell, on drums). In addition to guitar, Jimi plays eight-string bass (a rare Hagstrom) and a bit of piano, as coached by engineer Eddie Kramer. On this instructional CD, the sound of the eight-string bass was simulated by performing the bass lick octaves apart, on two separate tracks, and blending the two tracks together. During the guitar solo and outro, the piano part is simulated on guitar.

Figure 1 – Introduction

The intro lick (borrowed by Robin Trower for his own "Day of the Eagle") is based on C♯ minor pentatonic (C♯–E–F♯–G♯–B) and is played in unison by guitar and bass. This scale, in conjunction with the C# blues scale (C♯–E–F♯–G–G♯–B), is also utilized for all of the improvised soloing.

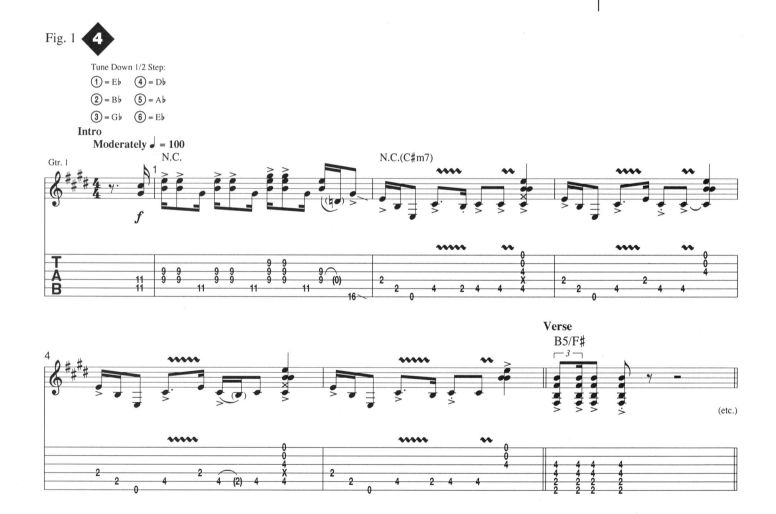

Figure 2 – Verse

The verse rhythm figure is based on a combination of power chords (in measures 1, 2, 4, 5, 6, and 8) and octaves (in measures 2, 3, 6, and 7). On the octave figures, Jimi gets a bit of the A string in between the octave shape formed on the low E and D strings, creating a different type of power chord, one that can be interpreted as positioning the fifth in the bass (e.g., in measure 3, the G♯ octave with the C♯ in the middle can be analyzed as C♯5/G♯).

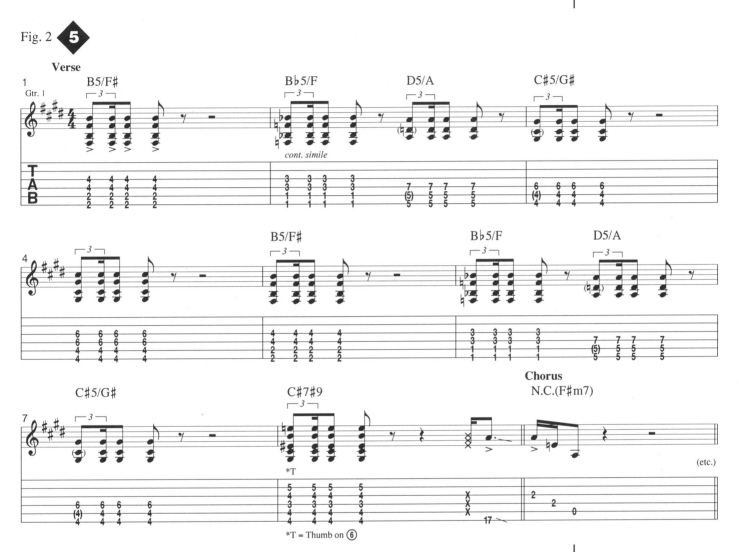

Figure 3 – Chorus

For the chorus, the main lick, originally played in C♯ minor, is transposed up to F♯ minor in measures 1 and 2, and is based on F♯ minor pentatonic (F♯–A–B–C♯–E). After a return to the lick in C♯, double-stop bends are played in measures 5 and 6, based on G♯ Dorian (G♯–A♯–B–C♯–D♯–E♯–F♯) and C♯ Dorian (C♯–D♯–E–F♯–G♯–A–B), respectively.

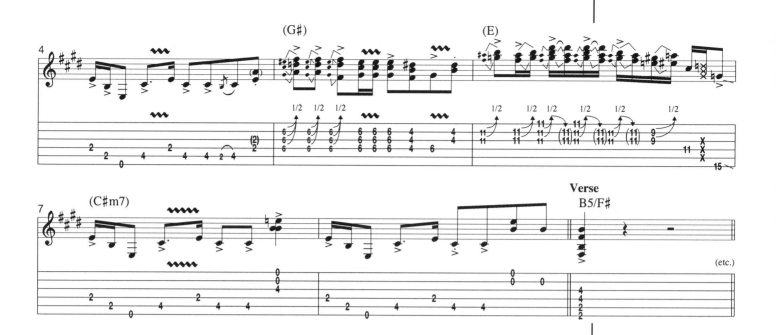

Figure 4 – Guitar Solo

The guitar solo begins in fourth position and quickly moves up to ninth position in measure 2. Jimi employs some unusual bends (the low C♯ [sixth string, ninth fret], the fifth, G♯ [fifth string, eleventh fret], and the "middle" C♯ [fourth string, eleventh fret]). For this solo, I used the red Dunlop Fuzz Face, which provides a bit more brightness than the blue Fuzz Face (which was used for the rhythm parts). Jimi's phrasing is quirky and hard to recreate throughout this solo, so read the rhythms carefully while listening to the solo both at the normal tempo and as played slowly. In the last three measures of the solo, Jimi employs very wide, two-step bends, recalling one of his heroes, blues master Albert King.

*Piano arr. for gtr.
**Chord symbols reflect implied tonality.

Chorus

N.C.(F#m7)

(etc.)

Figure 5 – Outro-Solo

Jimi's magnificent outro solo builds on much of the same material as the main solo, but here the phrases are even more complicated and aggressive. Measures 7–9 are particularly tricky, and, well, exquisitely Jimi Hendrix. The solo ends with a high E, repeatedly bent up to F# and released.

Fig. 5 **9** **10**

*Chord symbols reflect implied tonality.

*Piano arr. for gtr.

MANIC DEPRESSION
Words and Music by Jimi Hendrix

Know any other rock waltzes? Me neither. "Manic Depression" is one of Hendrix's best-loved tunes—a powerhouse of guitar-driven ferocity—and, though seemingly simple to play, is actually difficult to pull off with the same aggressive swagger and overall on-the-edge anxiety produced by the Experience. Though rarely played live, a wild version can be heard on *Live at Winterland* (Rykodisc).

Figure 6 – Introduction and Verse

The song begins with dramatic use of chromaticism, as D–D♯–E, played in even quarters, is contrasted against a complex drum fill and followed by the similarly chromatic G–G♯–A. The cornerstone one-measure signature riff, which commences at measure 3 of the intro, is played repeatedly and recurs throughout the piece.

The verse rhythm figure is built on single notes. Measure 8 alludes to A major pentatonic (A–B–C♯–E–F♯) with the use of the root (A), the third (C♯), and the fifth (E). Measure 9 alludes to G major pentatonic (G–A–B–D–E), again utilizing the root (G), third (B), and fifth (D), followed by a restatement of the intro figures. In measures 16 and 17, the root-3rd-5th shape is used over E and G, followed by single-note riffs that make reference to D, C, and G. Take note of the *drive* with which the entire figure is played.

Figure 7 – Guitar Solo

The guitar solo is actually preceded by a twelve-measure section, made up of an ascending melody performed with heavily vibratoed unison bends. The vibrato is slow, wide, and forceful, so be sure to vibrato from the wrist, *not* from the fingers. Measure 13 kicks off the bonafide 24-measure solo—one of Hendrix's greatest. Recreating these highly idiosyncratic, jam-and-cram phrases with absolute metronomic accuracy is very difficult; summoning up Jimi's *blood-of-fire* intensity is another matter entirely. The feeling of reckless abandon and skidding wildly out of control abounds, but Jimi somehow makes it all click like clockwork. This is *controlled chaos* at its best. The entire solo is based on A minor pentatonic (A–C–D–E–G), with subtle use of the ninth, B.

* 3rd finger bends C (3rd str./17th Fret), and also lightly frets G (4th str./17th fret), bending it 1/2 step. G (bent to G♯) feeds back, and is not picked.

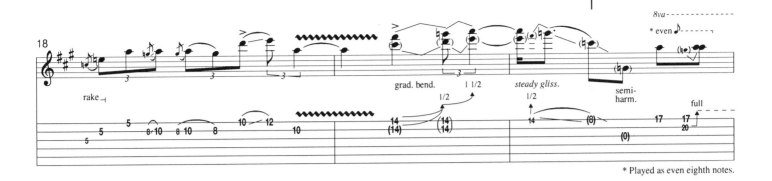

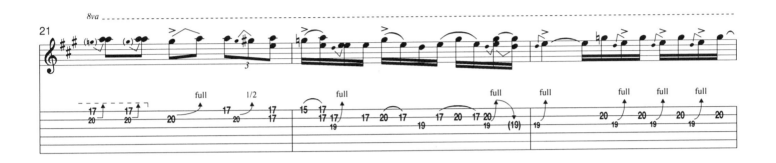

* Played as even eighth notes.

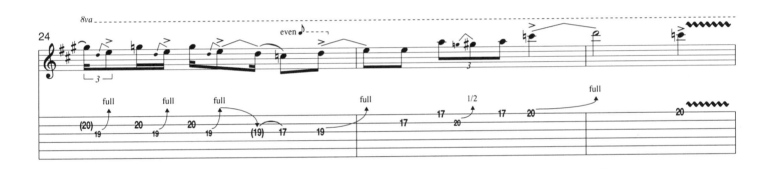

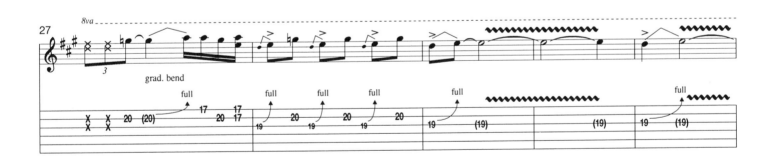

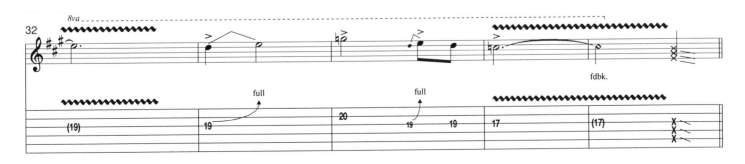

Figure 8 – Verse and Outro

All previous themes are repeated in this section, with unison bends added during the verse (measures 4-7 and 11-14). The intro stop-start riff is played repeatedly here, trading off with drum fills. The song ends with a little toggle switch-induced feedback.

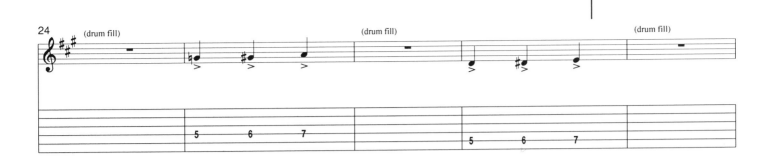

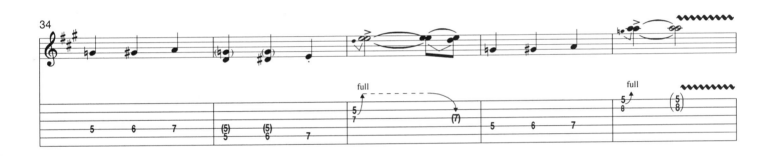

* Played as even eighth notes.

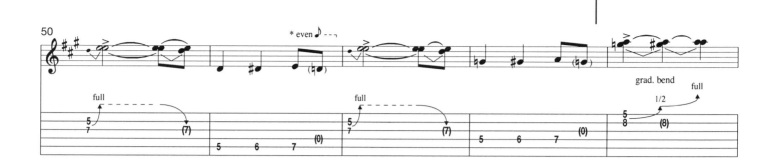

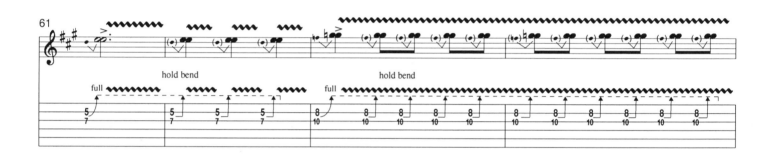

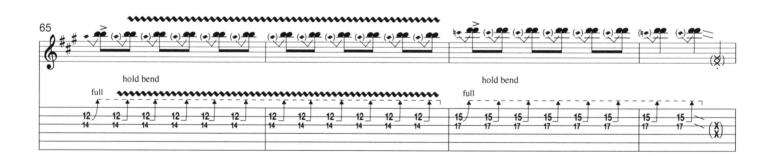

Free Time
A5

Fade Out

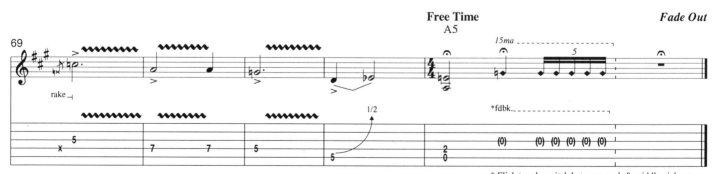

* Flick toggle switch between neck & middle pickups,
sounding feedback pitch (G) in specified rhythm.

HEY JOE
Words and Music by Billy Roberts

Written by west coast musician Billy Roberts and covered in '65 by the Leaves and in '66 by Tim Rose, "Hey Joe" became one of Hendrix's most well-known songs—one he turned into a rock anthem. By late '66, it was the Jimi Hendrix Experience's first U.K. hit.

Figure 9 – Intro and Verse

The song begins with a single-note riff based on E minor pentatonic (E–G–A–B–D), utilizing unison high Es (measure 1). Another E minor pentatonic figure sets up the verse "cycle of fifths" chord progression, C–G–D–A–E, which is played repeatedly for the remainder of the tune. Jimi pulls out all of his R&B/soul rhythm guitar mastery in the verse section, combining small chord voicings (two- and three-note forms), voice leading, and little single-note figures throughout. And the tone? Beautifully crystal-clear.

Notice in particular that the root notes of the G and A chords are usually fretted with the thumb; using the thumb in this way allowed Jimi the use of his index, middle, ring finger, and pinky for elaborate chordal work on the other strings. Abutting the primary rhythm guitar is a second rhythm guitar which plays mostly dead-string accents on beats 2 and 4 of each measure. This technique of accentuating the "backbeat" is another staple of R&B/soul guitar. This guitar also adds little single-note figures throughout. The thin tone of this guitar is achieved with the use of an "out-of-phase" toggle switch position, set between the neck and middle pickups.

Fig. 9

*Chord symbols reflect implied tonality.

*T = Thumb on ⑥

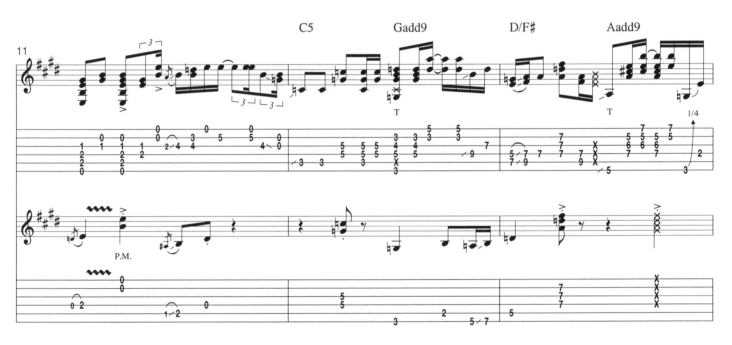

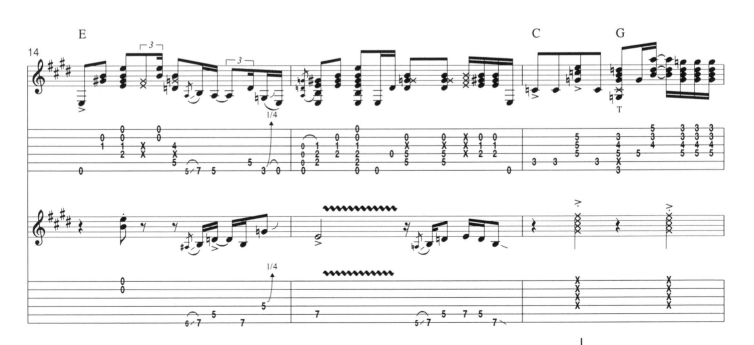

Figure 10 – Guitar Solo

Another true gem of a solo; Jimi often quoted himself when playing this song live. The solo is based entirely on E minor pentatonic (E–G–A–B–D) with the exception of the brief F♯s that appear in measure 7. My favorite moment in the whole solo? The stray open D string in measure 5, beat 3, second sixteenth. After careful study of the solo, give special scrutiny to the rhythm track as well. The solo ends with the mega-classic chromatic lick that links together all of the chords in the progression (measures 9 and 10).

Fig. 10 ⟨16⟩ ⟨17⟩

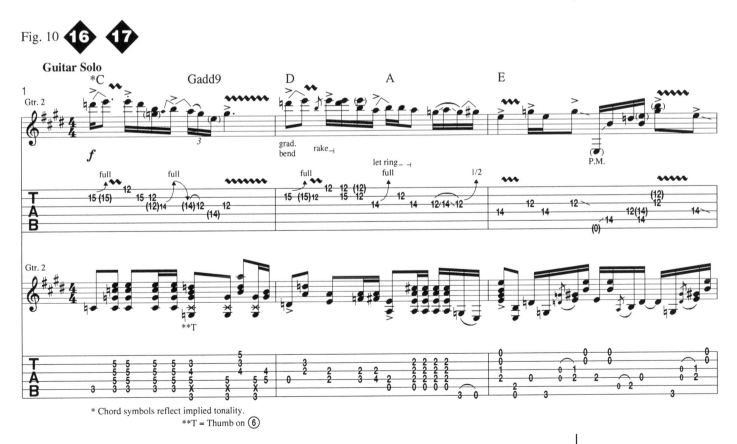

* Chord symbols reflect implied tonality.

**T = Thumb on ⑥

*T = Thumb on ⑥

THE WIND CRIES MARY

Words and Music by Jimi Hendrix

Figure 11 – Introduction

Jimi's mastery of rhythm guitar is evident from the start on this beautiful ballad, which kicks off with chromatically ascending root-fifth power chords—Eb5–E5–F5—with the fifth of each chord sounded "in the bass" (positioned as the lowest note in the chord voicing, also known as "second inversion" chord voicings). These chord voicings are used in measures 1 and 3. In measures 2 and 4, Jimi plays "first inversion" chords, which means that the third of each chord is sounded in the bass: Eb/G–E/G#–F/A. In measure 4, Jimi throws in a lick based on F major pentatonic (F–G–A–C–D), serving as a segue into the verse section. The rhythm guitar tone Jimi achieves is luscious—clean and clear, but with a warm "punch." Oh, what those vintage '66 Marshall Plexis can do!

Figure 12 – Verse

As in "Hey Joe," Jimi uses his thumb to fret the bass notes of many of the chords in this section, enabling him to use his other four fingers for intricate chordal improvisation. Stock techniques here are the G-to-A hammer-on over the F chord in measure 2, the C-to-D hammer-on over the F chord in measure 4, and the E-to-D pull-off over the G chord in measure 7. Examine the transcription and the recording closely to insure accurate recreation of this rhythm part.

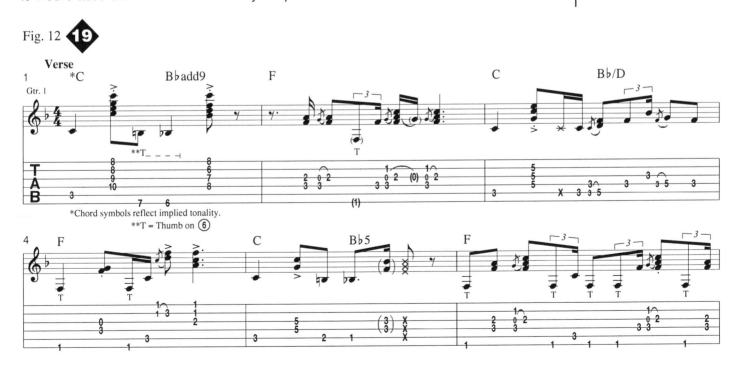

*Chord symbols reflect implied tonality.
**T = Thumb on ⑥

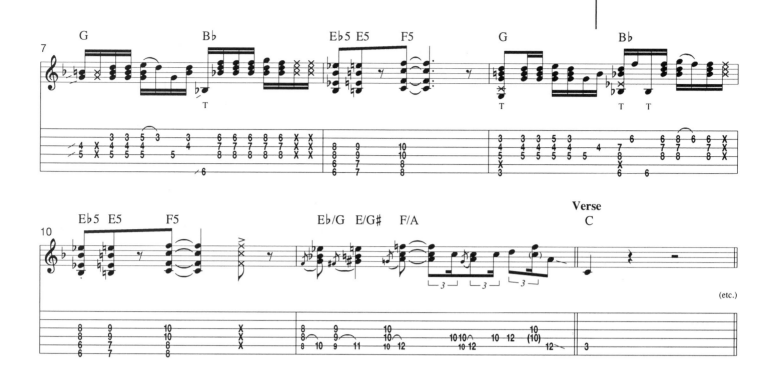

Figure 13 – Guitar Solo

Jimi's delicate solo (left channel) begins with six measures based on F major pentatonic (F–G–A–C–D) with abundant use of hammer-ons. Focus on the subtle differences between the grace-note hammers (as in measures 1–3) and the sixteenth-note hammers (as in measures 4 and 6).

In measures 7 and 8, Jimi plays similar hammer-on double-stop (two-note) figures. In measure 7 (over the G chord), the figures are based on G major pentatonic (G–A–B–D–E). In measure 8, Jimi adds the sixth, G, and the suspended 4th, Eb, to the Bb chord. Measure 9 features a riff based on Db minor pentatonic (Db–Fb–Gb–Ab–Cb), followed by a return to F major pentatonic.

For the rhythm guitar track (right channel), Jimi improvises freely through the new progression (F–Eb–Bb–Ab) with a single-note figure played in unison with the bass (measures 2, 4, and 6). Turn the balance control completely to the right for closer inspection of the rhythm part.

Fig. 13 **20** **21**

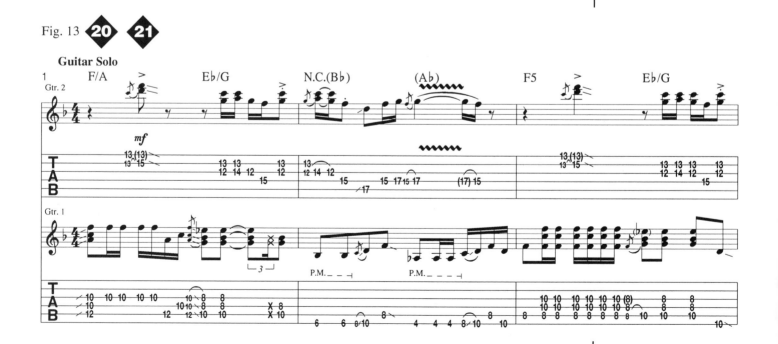

*T = Thumb on ⑥

Figure 14 – Outro

This excerpt begins at measure 10 of the fourth verse and encompasses the last eight measures of the tune. Again, the primary rhythm guitar is heard in the right channel, and the supplementary rhythm guitar (the one playing the fills) is heard in the left. The rhythm guitar repeats the basic two-measure rhythm figure, while the supplementary guitar plays fills based primarily on F major pentatonic (F–G–A–C–D).

Fig. 14 **22**

Outro

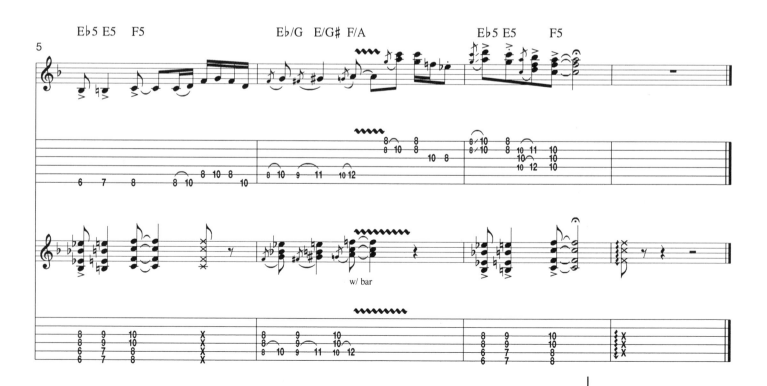

LITTLE WING

Words and Music by Jimi Hendrix

Figure 15 – Introduction

This classic intro serves further testimony to Hendrix's inventive genius as a rhythm guitarist, as he builds on R&B/soul rhythm guitar conventions to create his own other-worldly style. Like the supplementary guitar on "Hey Joe," Jimi utilizes an "out-of-phase" toggle switch position, set between the neck and middle pickups. In the pickup measure, the harmonic sounded on the D string, twelfth fret is highly incidental; don't worry if you have trouble sounding this harmonic along with the other pitches. It is important, however, to clearly sound the thumb-fretted low E note along with the more clearly articulated E and B on the top two strings.

Strive to attain as smooth a performance as possible as you shift back and forth between the single-note and chordal figures throughout this intro. A consistent attack with the picking hand is essential. Also, allow all notes to ring throughout.

Fig. 15

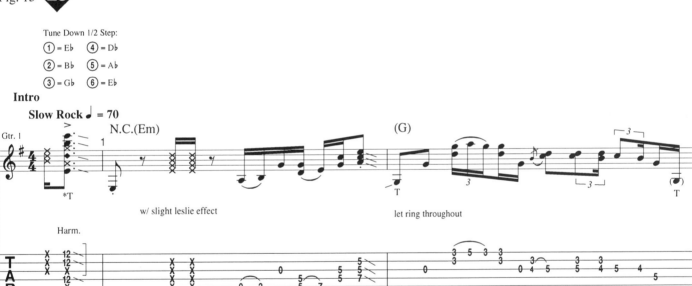

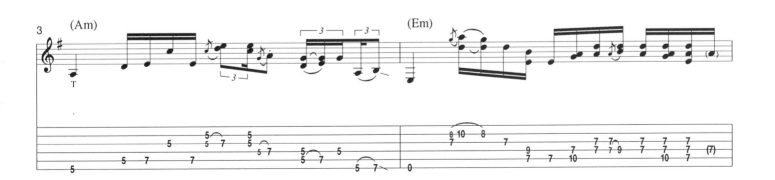

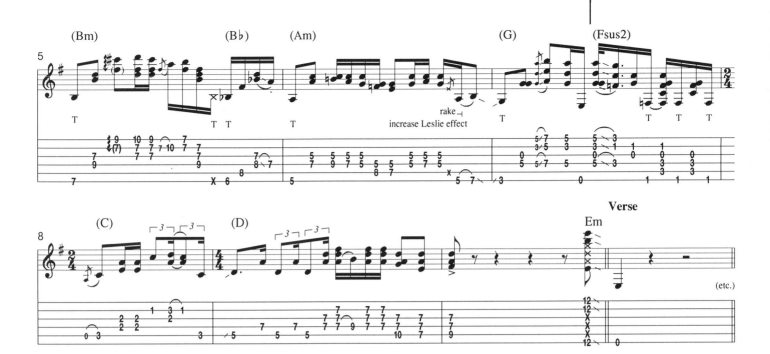

Figure 16 – First Verse

Jimi builds on the chordal-fragment concept during the verse sections of this tune. Once again, read through the transcription carefully, and listen closely to the recording. Every measure is a gem. Once you've got these figures down perfectly, add some twists and turns of your own.

Fig. 16

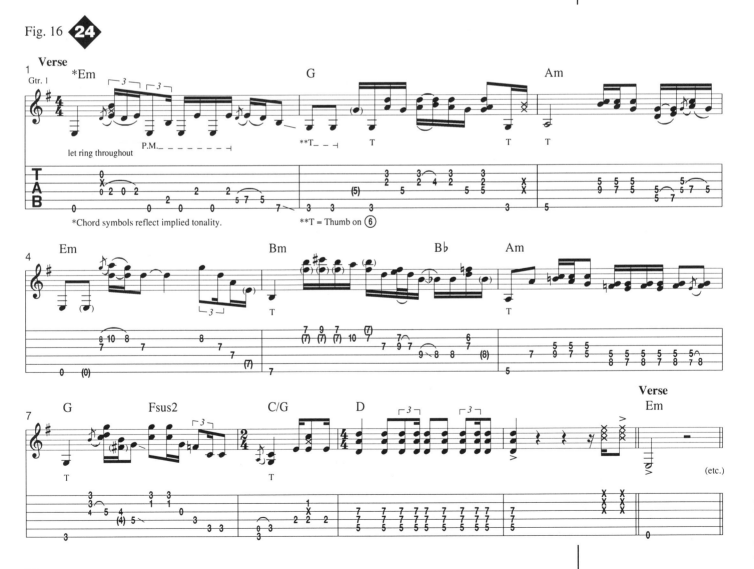

Figure 17 – Second Verse

Of the improvised rhythm work in this section, two measures in particular stand out—measure 1 and measure 6. In measure 1, Jimi plays a single-note figure across beats 3 and 4, based on E minor pentatonic (E–G–A–B–D), with the sixth, C♯, played in place of the seventh, D. The twist is that these single notes are played in conjunction with the open high E and B strings, providing a flowing, singing quality to the line. In measure 6, Jimi uses this same altered minor pentatonic scale, this time transposed to A (A–C–D–E–F♯), across beats 1 and 2, moving into two-note figures alluding to Csus2 and Csus4 across beats 3 and 4.

Fig. 17

Figure 18 – Outro-Guitar Solo

The mix during this solo section is unusual in that the rhythm guitar is hard-panned in *stereo*, hard right and left, while the lead guitar sits slightly off center, to the right. The rhythm guitar part is more aggressive than during the verse section, relying more on full chord forms. The slow, highly melodic lead guitar lines are based on E minor pentatonic (E–G–A–B–D) in measures 1–5, which can also be interpreted as G major pentatonic (G–A–B–D–E) when played over the G chord, in measure 2. Notice that E minor pentatonic and G major pentatonic are made up of the same notes, but start at different points in the series.

All tracks are treated with a Leslie/rotating speaker effect. This track fades out a little later than on the original recording; this was done to facilitate hearing the solo all the way through to the absolute fade.

Fig. 18

Outro-Guitar Solo

*Chord symbols reflect implied tonality   **T = Thumb on ⑥

*slight vibrato

CASTLES MADE OF SAND
Words and Music by Jimi Hendrix

Figure 19 – Introduction

This introduction features more Hendrix rhythm guitar work of the trailblazing, mind-boggling variety. The song opens with a "free time" feeling (in time, but played very freely) as "sus2" chords (also thought of as "add9/no 3rd" chords) are slid up and down the neck, alluding to the tonal structure of a G minor pentatonic scale (G–B♭–C–D–F). This unique chord voicing is a Hendrix trademark; you'll find it in other Hendrix classics such as "Little Wing," "The Wind Cries Mary," and "Fire" to name but a few. An octave shape is formed with the thumb-fretted root note (sixth string) and the middle-finger-fretted root one octave higher (fourth string). Add to this the fifth, fretted with the index finger on the second string, and the ninth (or second), fretted with the pinky on the high E string.

Hendrix then moves into beautiful single-note and double-stop figures that allude to a G–Bm(or Gmaj9)–C–B♭6–G–Gm(or B♭)–C–B♭ chord progression. Learning this classic intro is a must for any true Hendrix devotee.

Fig. 19

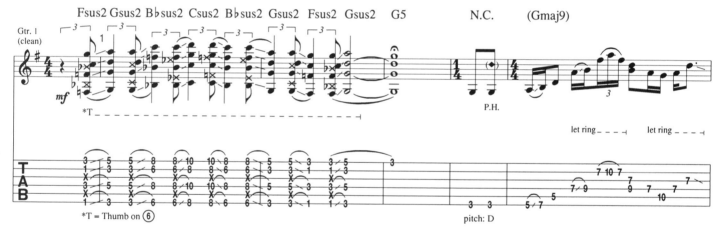

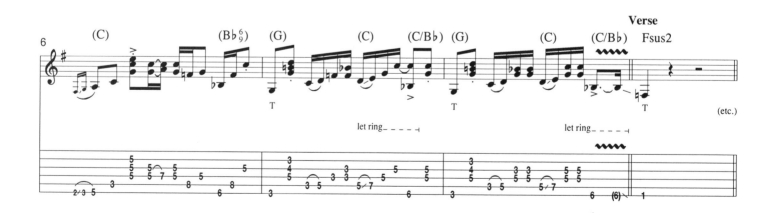

Figure 20 – Verse

Jimi once again employs his trademark chordal-fragment style of rhythm guitar, moving freely between single-note figures, double-stops, and triple-stops. Notice that Jimi *never* plays a conventional full-voiced chord! The closest he comes is the Em7 voicing that appears in measure 3. (The incidental backwards guitar played on the original recording throughout this section has been omitted.)

Figure 21 – First Chorus

This excerpt begins with the final two measures of the first verse, as the last measure of the verse section serves as a pickup into the chorus section. The chorus rhythm figure is essentially the same as what Jimi first introduced in measures 4-7 of the intro, but he adds interesting twists and turns throughout. Compare the two rhythm parts and notice the similarities and differences between what Jimi plays here and what was played for the intro.

Fig. 21 **30**

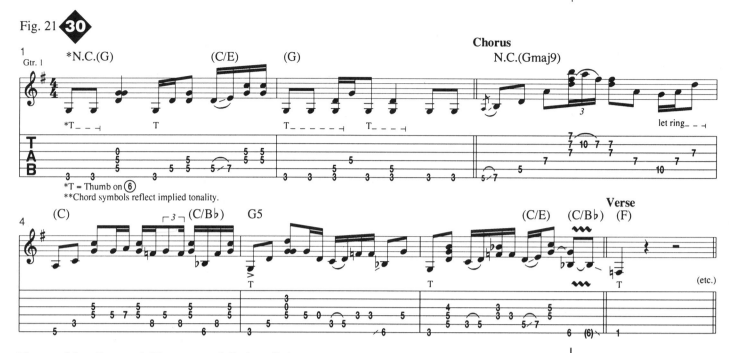

Figure 22 – Second Chorus and Guitar Solo

As heard in a few of the other tunes, the rhythm guitar is positioned in the right channel, and the lead guitar is positioned in the left channel. For the rhythm part, Jimi elaborates slightly on previously played figures; his consistently brilliant inventiveness is something to behold.

The guitar solo on the original recording of this song is backwards. When recording the solo, Jimi flipped the master tape over, allowing him to hear the entire track backwards. He then played normally to the backwards track, recording a track of lead guitar. The tape was then flipped over again, so that now, the backing track plays forwards, and the solo track plays backwards. Got it? This is a technique possible only with analog tape machines, as it is not possible to flip the tape over and record in the opposite direction on digital machines.

For this instructional vehicle, I've arranged the backwards solo for forwards guitar, allowing one to recreate the backwards phrases (and simulate the backwards effect) while playing normally. The true attack and decay of a backwards track (the prime ingredient in a backwards track) is not attainable in this way, however. You could try a volume pedal to create a similar effect, or, for the wealthy, try an Eventide Ultra-Harmonizer, which offers a "backwards guitar" patch. You could also try an Electro-Harmonix 16-second delay (quite rare), which will reproduce backwards whatever you play.

Fig. 22 **31** **32**

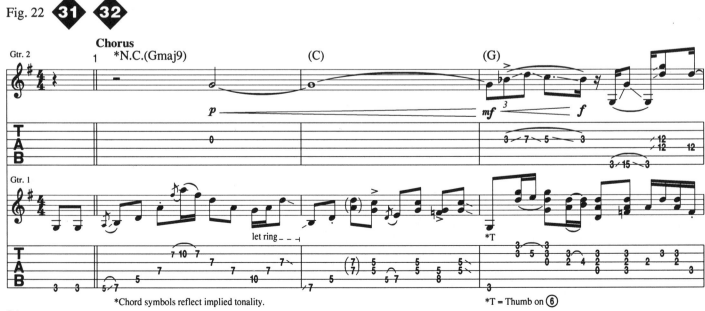

Figure 23 – Outro

For the outro, the "free" feeling of the intro is restated, only this time it's much looser. Similar guitar figures are used (watch closely for the slight discrepancies), and the segment ends with a restatement of the sliding "sus2" chords heard on the intro. Notice that the toggle switch is moved from "out-of-phase" to the middle pickup just prior to the sliding chords. As in the "Little Wing" segment, this excerpt does not fade out as severely as heard on the original recording.

Fig. 23 **33**

*T = Thumb on ⑥
**Chord symbols reflect implied tonality.

*After picking these notes, switch from "out-of-phase" toggle switch position (between neck & middle pickups) to middle pickup only.

FIRE
Words and Music by Jimi Hendrix

Figure 24 – Introduction

This perennial fave rave-up begins with an octave guitar figure based on the D blues scale (D–F–G–A♭–A–C). Often interpreted incorrectly, the phrase begins on beat 4 of the pickup measure (with the A♭ octave quarter note), followed by a G octave quarter note played squarely on beat 1 of measure 1.

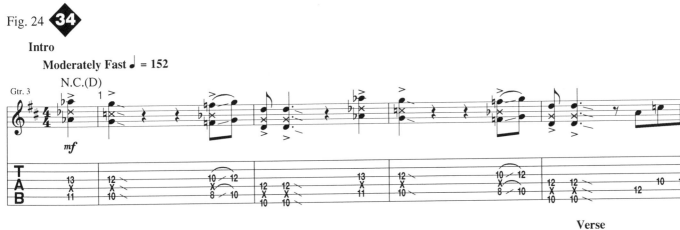

Figure 25 – Verse

The verse guitar part of "Fire" is simple: a repeated single-note phrase based on D minor pentatonic (D–F–G–A–C). Jimi ends the section with a D minor pentatonic riff that slides up one whole step, transforming itself into a D major pentatonic (D–E–F♯–A–B) riff. (On the original recording, there is a very subtle guitar overdub which sits right on top of the main guitar part; it has been omitted here.)

Figure 26 – Chorus

Jimi plays "thumbed" major chords (sixth-string root notes fretted with the thumb) throughout this section, adding the 9th on the high E string (fretted with the pinky) to the D and C chords. In measures 2, 6, and 8, single-note licks based on D minor pentatonic are played; in measure 4, a single-note lick based on D major pentatonic is played. The section ends with a restatement of the verse lick.

Fig. 26 **36**

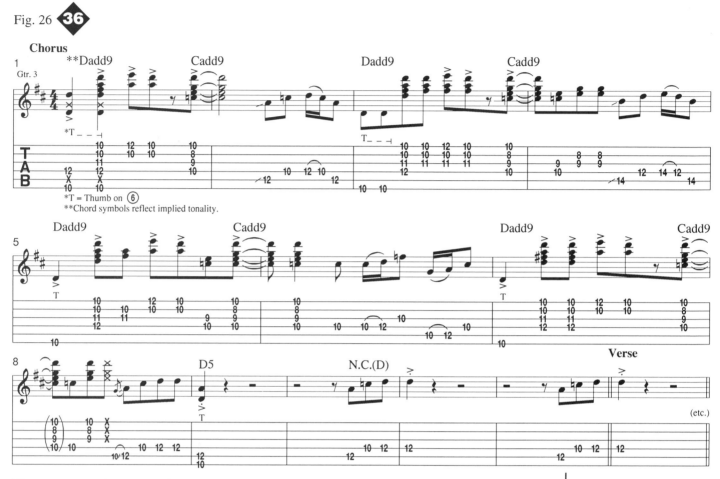

Figure 27 – Bridge and Guitar Solo

The bridge features full-voiced major chords over which Hendrix pleads, "Move over, Rover, and let *Jimi* take over!" (The genesis of the song clarifies the meaning of this plea. Arriving at bassist Noel Redding's mother's house in Folkstone, England for Christmas in 1966, Jimi was cold and asked if he could "stand next to her fire." The German shepherd was in his way, so…)

The solo section features three guitar parts: one rhythm (hard right) and two leads—one treated with Octavia (left channel) and one heavily distorted (right channel). To hear the rhythm guitar part more clearly, listen to the right channel only. The two leads virtually double each other, but there are some very cool discrepancies. The lines are based on E minor pentatonic (E–G–A–B–D). Each of these parts is played slowly to a click track for more thorough examination.

Fig. 27 **37** **38** **39**

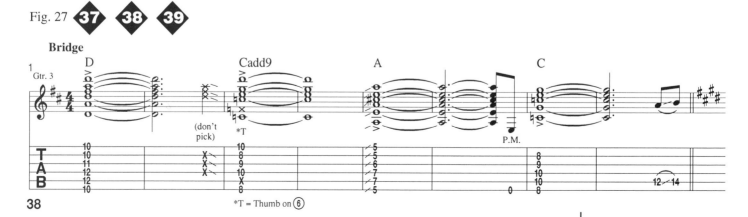

Guitar Solo

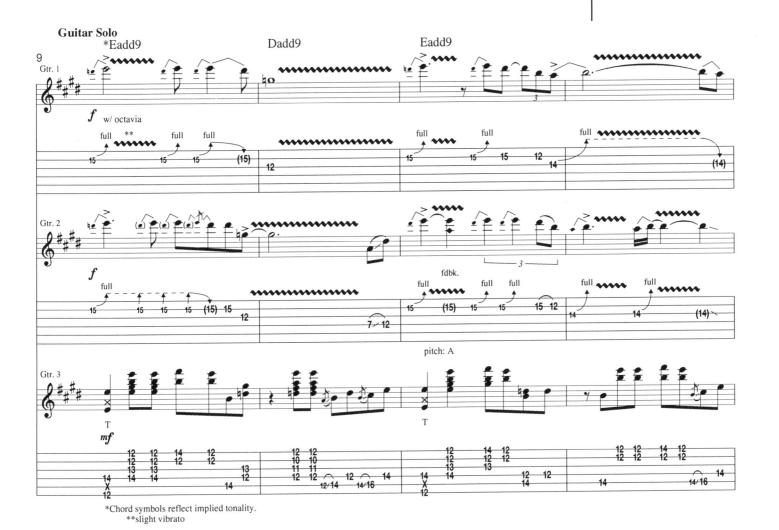

*Chord symbols reflect implied tonality.
**slight vibrato

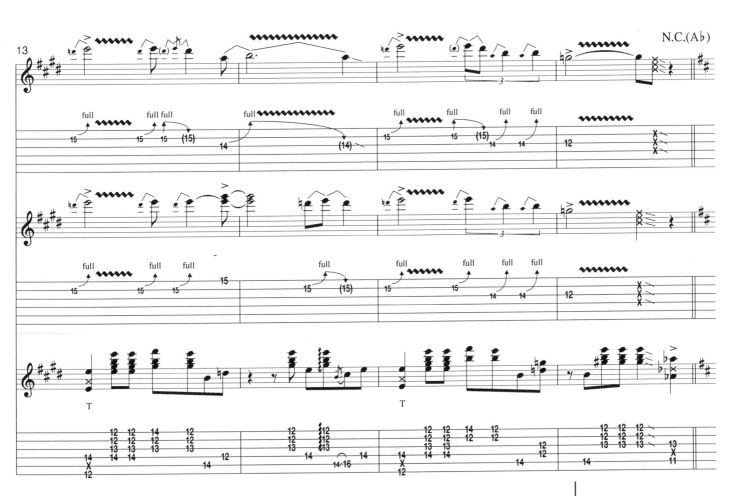

Figure 28 – Outro-Guitar Solo

The "Fire" outro is very similar to the solo section, except here the song moves back and forth between D and E, with four measures of each played alternately. This excerpt actually begins with the last four measures of the final chorus, played in D, before moving into the outro, where the song shifts up one whole step to E. Three guitars are again featured (two lead, one rhythm), panned similarly. Check out the slow versions of the solos for closer scrutiny.

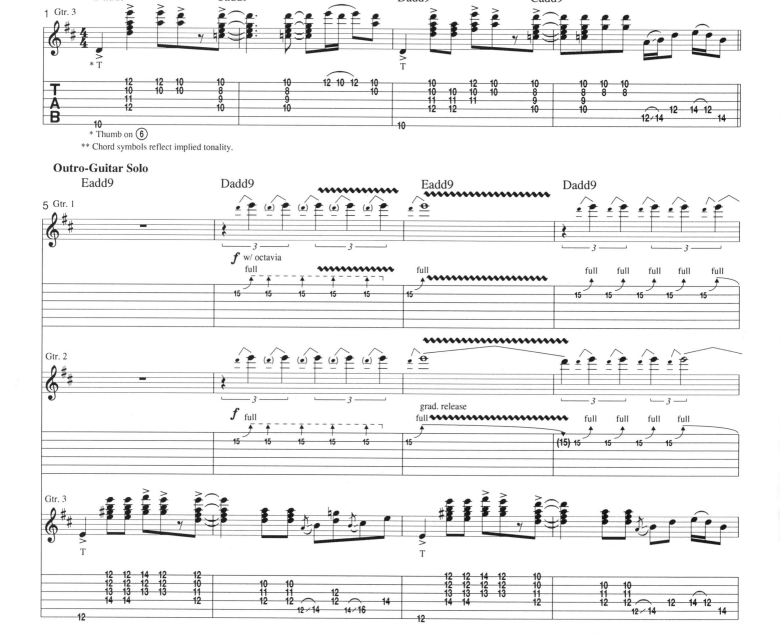

PURPLE HAZE

Words and Music by Jimi Hendrix

Figure 29 – Introduction

Another oft-misinterpreted lick, the "Purple Haze" intro is performed by combining an alternating octave Bb figure, played on guitar, with an alternating octave E figure, played on the bass. The combination of these two parts creates an intervallic relationship known as a *tritone*, because the distance between Bb and E is three whole steps (tri=three, tone=whole tone).

In measures 3–10, Jimi plays the signature single-note figure based on E minor pentatonic (E–G–A–B–D). Notice all of the subtleties in the way the phrases are articulated—herein lies the true beauty. In measures 4, 6, and 8, a second guitar adds a heavily attacked G note (sixth string, fifteenth fret), played on beat 4 and immediately (and dramatically) slid down the neck. A Fuzz Face is used on both guitar tracks.

In measures 11–14, Jimi moves from his signature E7♯9 chord (previously famous for its use in the song "Hold It" by Bill Doggett) to G and A major chords, voiced with "thumbed" root notes on the 6th string.

Fig. 29

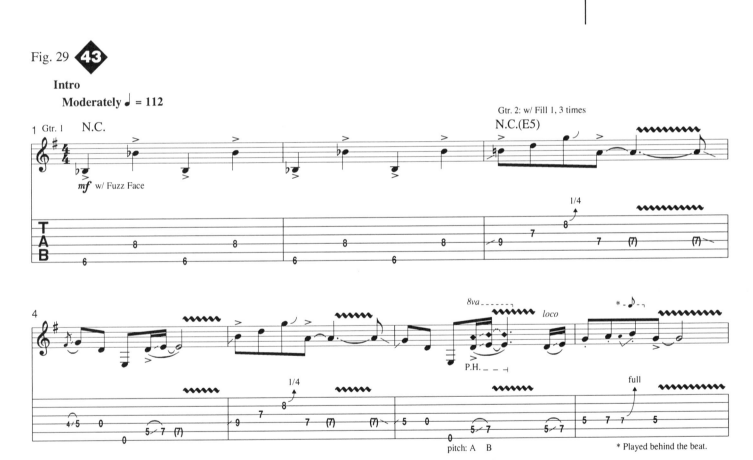

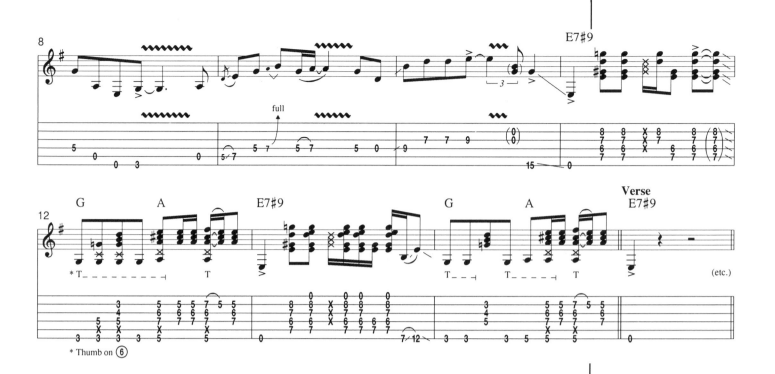

Figure 30 – Verse

The same chord figure played in measures 11–14 of the intro (E7#9–G–A) is used for the first six measures of the verse. Following the "stop-time" figure in measure 7, measure 8 features the use of a sliding octave figure, followed by an E minor pentatonic melody doubled by the bass.

Fig. 30 **44**

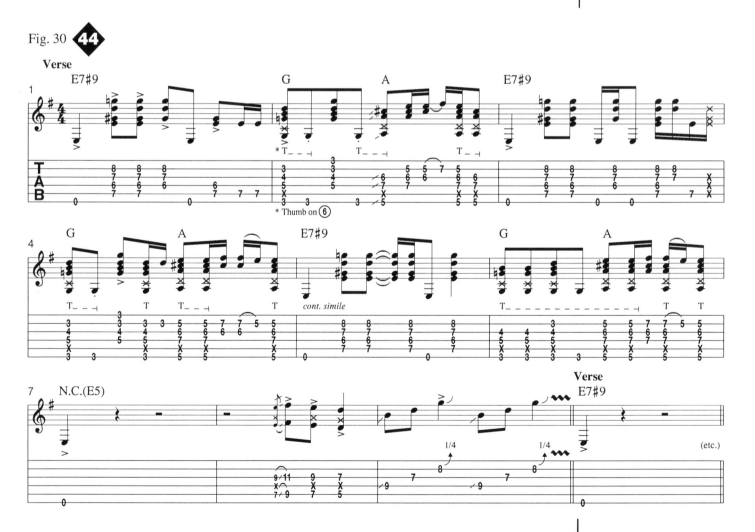

Figure 31 – Guitar Solo

The end of verse two features a three-measure section—moving from A to B to D—designed to carry the listener back into the E minor tonality of the solo section. In the first measure, the single-note melody is based on E major pentatonic (E–F♯–G♯–B–C♯) and, as it is played over A, alludes also to A major pentatonic (A–B–C♯–E–F♯). In measures 2 and 3, Jimi moves back to E minor pentatonic.

The guitar solo is based on a combination of E Mixolydian (E–F♯–G♯–A–B–C♯–D) and E Dorian (E–F♯–G–A–B–C♯–D). Notice that the only difference between these two scales is the third scale degree: E Mixolydian is a major mode, and includes the major third, G♯; E Dorian is a minor mode, and includes the minor third, G.

Jimi's phrasing is a bit quirky and unpredictable here, as he makes allusions to Indian (as in Far East) classical music. The Octavia, an octave-splitting device designed by gadget guru Roger Mayer, is heard in all of its glory on this solo. To recreate the solo on this CD, I was lucky enough to acquire a vintage Octavia.

Fig. 31 ◆45◆ ◆46◆

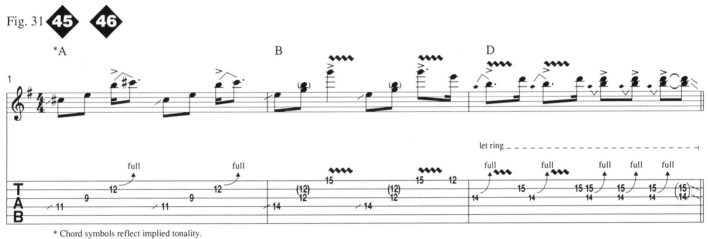

* Chord symbols reflect implied tonality.

Guitar Solo

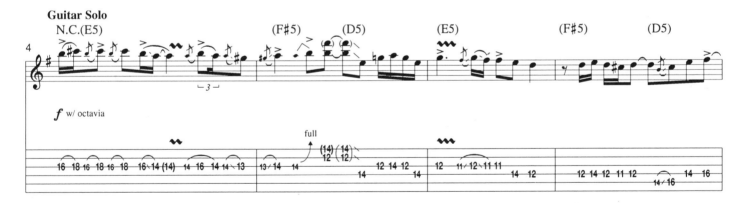

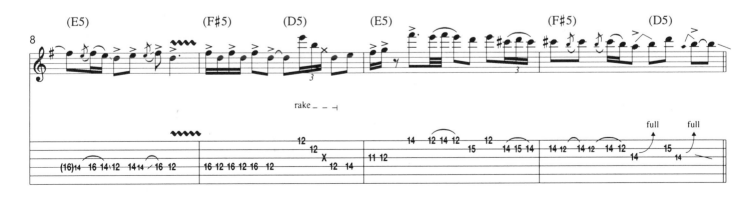

Figure 32 – Outro

This section begins at the same relative spot as the solo section, at measure 10 of the third verse. The difference here is that there are two distinct guitar parts—the basic rhythm guitar, and the Octavia guitar, as heard on the solo. For the rhythm guitar, everything after measure 5 is random improvisation, beginning with a trill (as shown) and succeeded by ad lib tremolo bar diving. The lead guitar essentially picks a high D, bent one whole step up to E, repeatedly, creating some unusual rhythmic groupings. Use what is written here as a guide; feel free to play similar figures of your own. Again, the pan presented here is wider than on the original.

On the original recording, similar lead guitar figures are played, recorded with the track at half-speed, which results in the figures sounding twice as fast when the track is played at normal speed. These "cellophane typewriter" guitars have been omitted in this instructional recording.

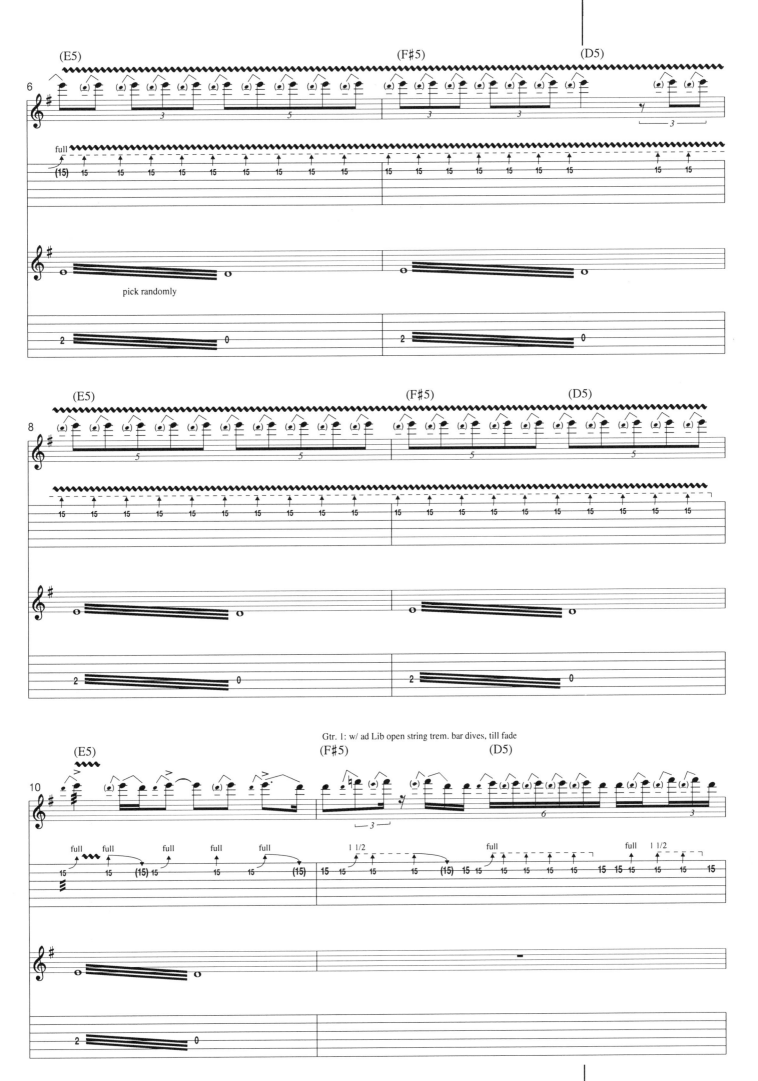

Gtr. 1: w/ ad Lib open string trem. bar dives, till fade

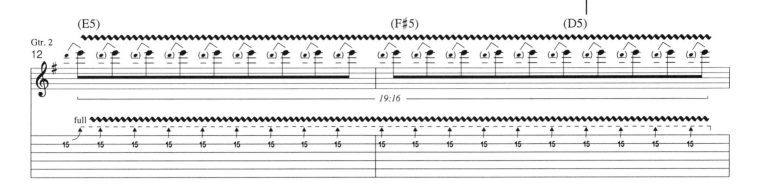

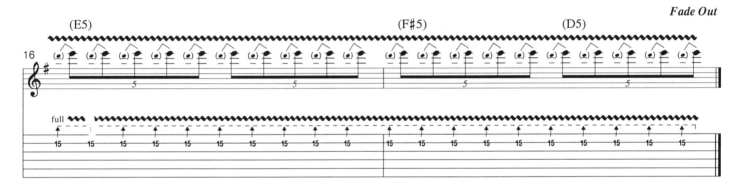

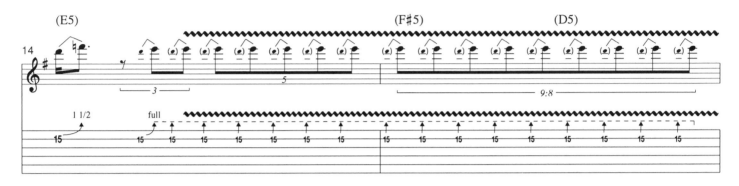

RED HOUSE

Words and Music by Jimi Hendrix

Figure 33 – Introduction

This is Jimi Hendrix's only twelve-bar blues original, but it is an absolute classic and is probably played at more jam sessions than "(I Can't Get No) Satisfaction."

The first lick (in measures 1 and 2) is based on a dominant seventh shape. In measure 1, it is a B7 chord shape, spelled (low to high) F♯, A, and D♯. There is no root note (B) in this chord voicing. In measure 2, this shape moves down one half step to B♭7, spelled (low to high) F, A♭, and D. There is no root note (B♭) in this voicing, either. In measure 3, Jimi repeatedly bends an A (B string, tenth fret) up one whole step to B, and adds wide, slow vibrato. On each bend, he gets a little of the G and D strings under his ring finger, which is bending the B string. These other pitches may be incidental, but they add plenty of *vibe*. Simulate this phenomenon if you can.

Starting at measure 4, all of the improvisation is based on either B minor pentatonic (B–D–E–F♯–A) or B major pentatonic (B–C♯–D♯–F♯–G♯). Measures 4–7 are based on B minor pentatonic (in measure 4, Jimi adds the ninth, C♯), and measures 8–10 are based on B major pentatonic. Jimi's phrasing is beautifully liquid throughout, creating many rhythmic complexities. Count each phrase slowly and carefully, and study the slow versions of each chorus extensively. The guitar signal is treated with slap-back echo.

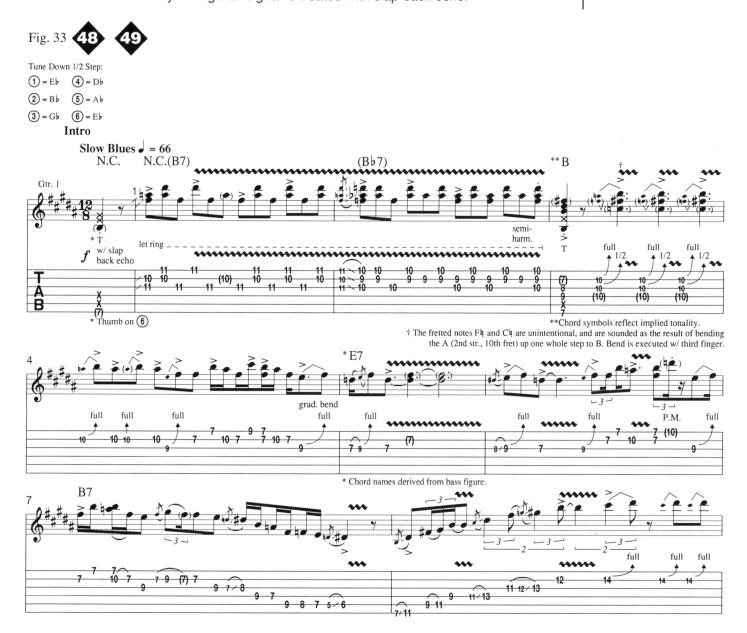

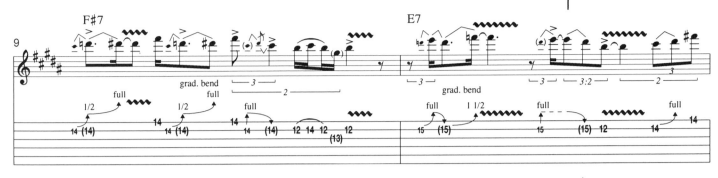

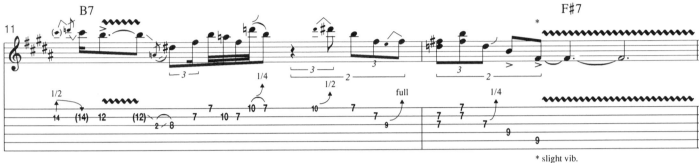

* slight vib.

Figure 34 – First Verse

During the verse sections of "Red House," Jimi plays little in the way of rhythm guitar when backing up his singing. Between his vocal phrases, however, he does a lot of improvised soloing. In measures 3 and 4, Jimi plays an incredible riff (based on B minor pentatonic) that starts, stops, starts, stops again, and then culminates in a group of slow phrases that are rhythmically and melodically unique. His main influences may have been Albert, Freddie, and B.B. King, but this type of guitar playing can only be attributed to Hendrix's own genius.

In measures 7 and 8, Jimi plays lines based on the B blues scale (B–D–E–F–F#–A), and in measure 9, he throws in a little E major pentatonic (E–F#–G#–B–C#) to anticipate the upcoming E chord in measure 10. In measures 11 and 12, Jimi plays lines that allude to B major pentatonic.

Figure 35 – Second Verse

After deft use of grace notes in measure 1, Jimi plays a stunning improvised line across measures 3 and 4, based primarily on B minor pentatonic but with the inclusion of the ninth, C♯ (second half of beat 4 in measure 3). In the second half of measure 4, he reverts back to the B blues scale, rounding off this beautiful lick. The lick across measures 7 and 8 features unison bends combined with a high B in measure 7, and the entire lick is based on B minor pentatonic. In measures 9 and 10, he adds sliding double-stops, sixths apart, alluding to both F♯7 and E7 chords, respectively. In measures 11 and 12, he plays another rhythmically deceptive phrase, again based on B minor pentatonic.

Figure 36 – Guitar Solo

To start the solo, Jimi kicks on his Fuzz Face distortion unit but only utilizes it for the first two licks, across measures 1–3. At measure 4, he turns it off and leaves it off (curiously, till the very last lick played in the tune). This opening phrase is based on B minor pentatonic, up in tenth position, with Jimi supplying fast repeated triplets, beginning at beat 4 of measure 2 and continuing into beat 1 of measure 3. At beat 2, he deftly shifts down to seventh position B minor pentatonic while in mid-phrase (an old B.B. King trick).

Across measures 4 and 5, Jimi settles into another fast, repeated lick, this time in seventh position; this lick has since become so overused that it is probably the biggest cliché in all of rock guitar soloing. (Jimmy Page used the same lick to wrap up his "Stairway to Heaven" solo—need I say any more?) In measures 6 and 7, as well as half of measure 8, Jimi plays phrases that almost defy being written down, due to the rhythmic complexity and subtlety. I highly recommend the digestion of small bites (one or two beats at a time) with careful listening to the slowed-down version of this segment. The lines are based on B minor pentatonic, again with the inclusion of the ninth, C# (a staple of another blues hero of Hendrix's, T-Bone Walker).

In the second half of measure 8, Jimi plays an awkward riff that serves to shift his fretting hand up to fourteenth position, followed by a B minor pentatonic riff in measure 9 that is rhythmically bizarre, but with its own innate sense of musical logic. The first half of measure 10 is based on B minor pentatonic, followed in the second half by B major pentatonic, and measures 11 and 12 round out this classic solo with B minor pentatonic phrases. All in all, a workout and a half.

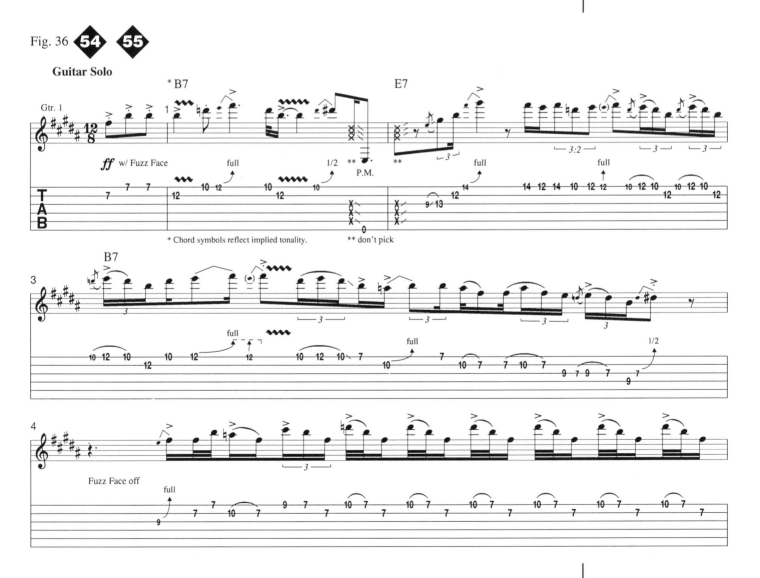

Fig. 36 **54** **55**

Guitar Solo

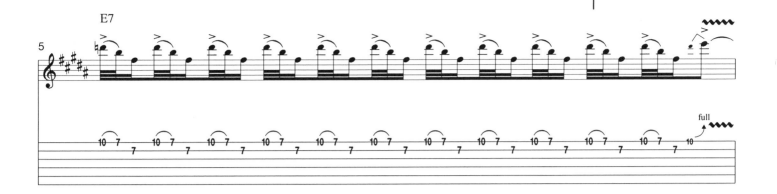

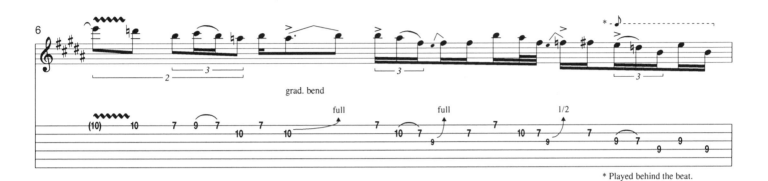

* Played behind the beat.

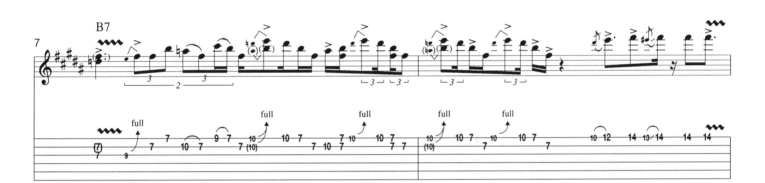

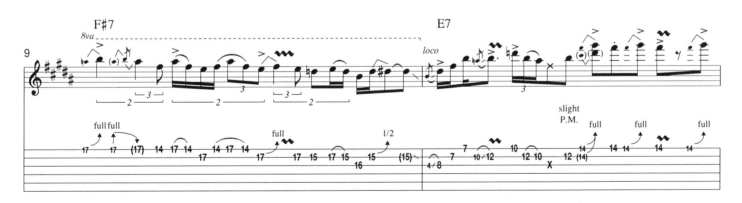

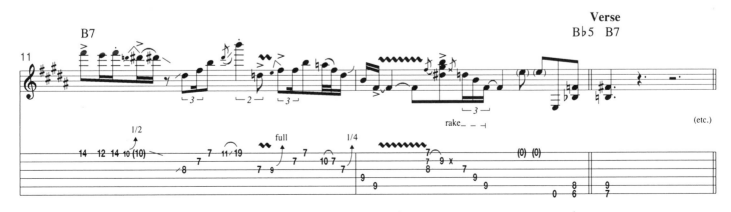

Figure 37 – Third Verse

Measures 1 and 2 feature the use of sliding double-stops, a sixth apart, followed in measures 3 and 4 with B minor pentatonic phrases that allude to B major (with the inclusion of the sixth, G♯, and the major third, D♯). Measure 7 (and the first half of measure 8) reintroduces the B7 voicing used at the head of the tune, this time strummed (and tremolo picked) aggressively, followed by a rhythmically complex (and hard to recreate) phrase based on B minor pentatonic.

The song ends with a one-measure lick most closely related to B major pentatonic, followed by a 6/8 measure, inserted to accommodate the chromatically descending C7–B7 ending figure, as the song shifts into "free time." Jimi's very last lick (w/ Fuzz Face) begins with B major pentatonic, and ends, somewhat ominously, with B minor pentatonic.

Fig. 37

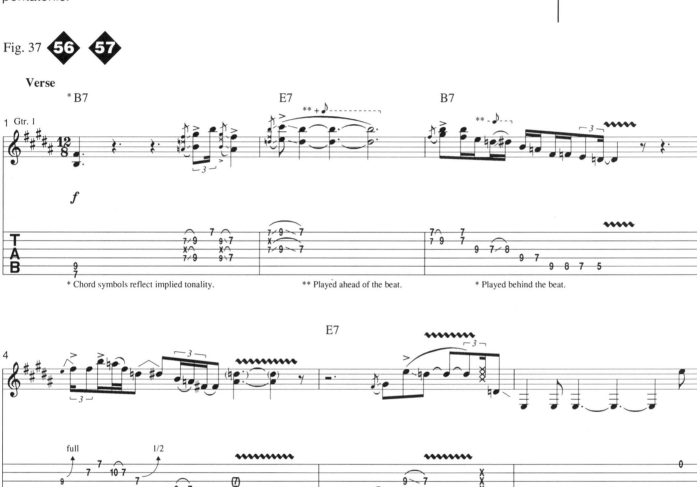

* Chord symbols reflect implied tonality.   ** Played ahead of the beat.   * Played behind the beat.

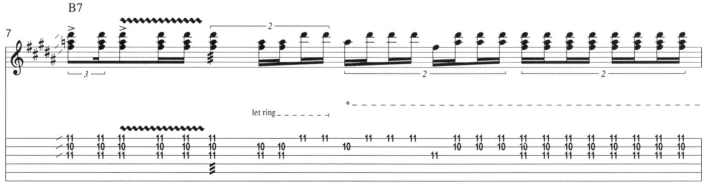

* slow tremolo picking

54

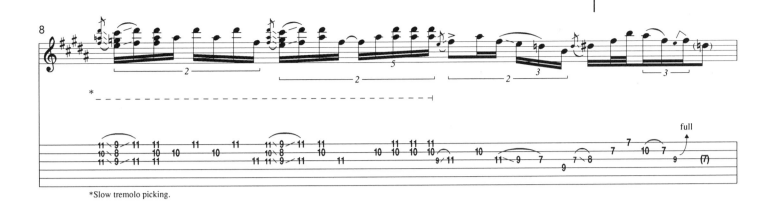

*Slow tremolo picking.

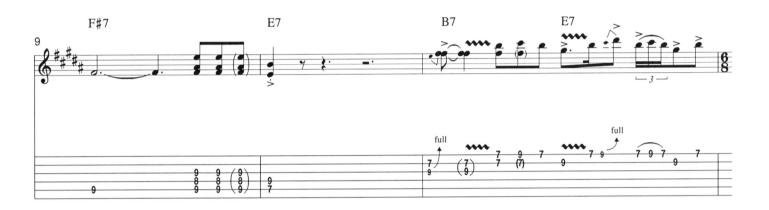

Free Time

P.M.

w/ Fuzz Face

FOXEY LADY
Words and Music by Jimi Hendrix

Figure 38 – Introduction and Verse

"Foxey Lady" features a one-of-a-kind intro: in "free time," Jimi vibratos an F (third string, tenth fret), which is bent one half step up to F♯, fretted with the index finger. The note is *not* picked but sounds due to the constant friction of the vibrato. While articulating this vibrato, the A note (second string, tenth fret) is caught under the index finger and also begins to sound due to friction. Subsequently, the A note swells into feedback, after which time is established with an aggressive "BOOoooo" down the G string, signifying beat 4 of the pickup measure.

The intro rhythm figure is similar to "Spanish Castle Magic," as a m7 chord (F♯m7 in this case) is played by first sounding the low root note, followed by the high ♭7th and ♭3rd at the top of the voicing. On beat 4 of measures 4 and 6, Jimi throws in B major chords. An overdubbed guitar adds double-stop accents (and trills) on beats 2 and 4, similar in concept to the dead-string "chugs" heard during the verse sections of "Hey Joe."

During the verse, Jimi continues the same basic rhythm pattern heard on the intro.

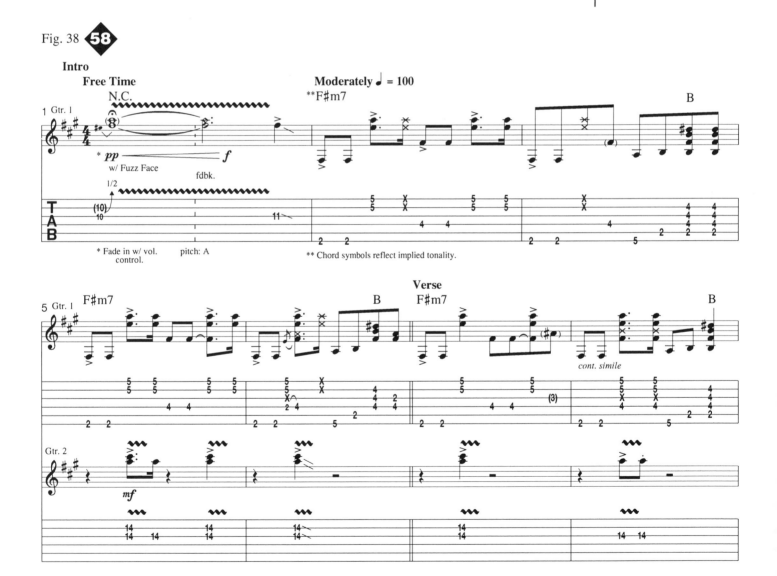

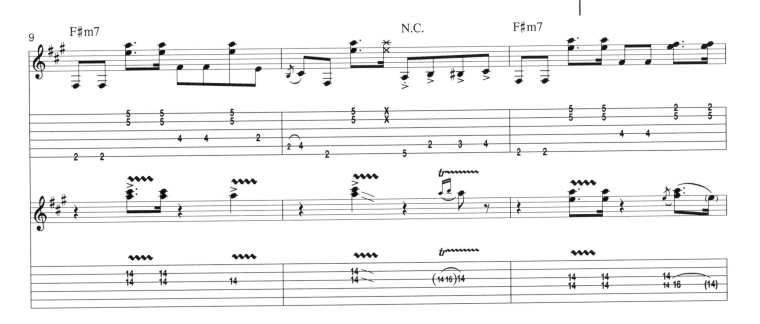

Figure 39 – Chorus

The guitar part during the chorus is one of the simplest parts Jimi ever laid down (he rarely chose the easy way): straight F# and E major chords are played throughout, with little single-note licks thrown in on beats 3 and 4 of every other measure. The lick across beats 3 and 4 in measure 6 is based on F# major pentatonic (F#–G#–A#–C#–D#). This is followed by a restatement of the verse rhythm figures of Gtrs. 1 and 2.

Fig. 39 **59**

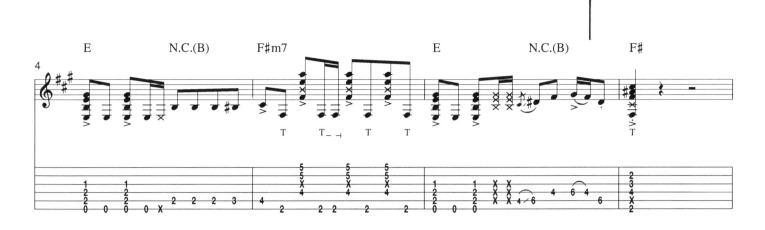

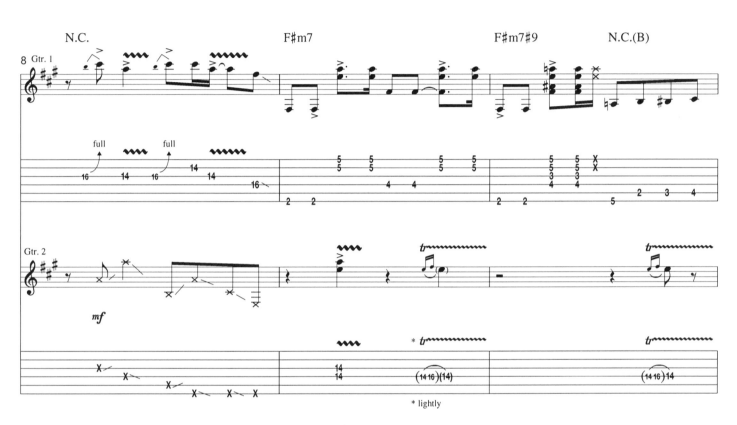

* lightly

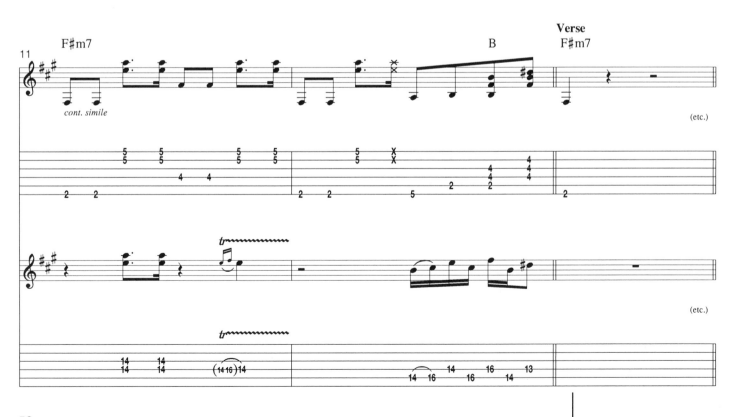

Figure 40 – Guitar Solo

Over the same basic rhythm pattern heard on the verse sections, Jimi plays an inspired solo based entirely on F♯ minor pentatonic (F♯–A–B–C♯–E). Unusual twists include the bending of the major 7th, F, up one half step to F♯ (measure 3), and the bending of the root, F♯, up one whole step to G♯ (measure 4). Also of note is the unique use of unison bends in measures 7-9.

* Chord symbols reflect implied tonality.

* T = Thumb on ⑥

Figure 41 – Outro

The "Foxey Lady" outro is really just an extended take on the verse guitar figures with slight improvisation added throughout. The song ends on a held B major chord, over which Gtr. 2 supplies a forceful microphone stand slide. (Be sure to step on the base of the stand before pushing the guitar strings against it; the stand has to be secure to insure constant friction.)

* Chord symbols reflect implied tonality.

* T = Thumb on ⑥

** Slow slide w/ microphone stand.

VOODOO CHILD (Slight Return)

Words and Music by Jimi Hendrix

This *tour-de-force* is one of Hendrix's crowning achievements—a clear and undeniable testament to his greatness as an artist. Though Jimi dismissed it as something "tossed off in the studio for the TV cameras," it remains as vital and earth-shaking today as the day it was recorded (May 3, 1968, to be exact).

Figure 42 – Introduction

This song fades in with solo guitar, as Jimi lightly strums muted strings while slowly rocking the wah-wah pedal back and forth. The wah is in bass position on beats 1 and 3, and is rocked to treble position on beats 2 and 4. After the 3/4 measure (measure 4), Jimi plays the signature melody, based on E minor pentatonic (E–G–A–B–D). At this point, the wah is rocked from bass to treble position on each downbeat.

Following this eight-measure figure, the wah is turned off and the whole band enters, as Jimi smashes violently into the second signature rhythm figure, made up of E major chords combined with single-note phrases based on E minor pentatonic. At the end of measure 16, a phrase is initiated as A (third string, second fret) is bent one whole step up to B, with the wah kicked on to full treble simultaneously. While holding the bent A and keeping the wah in full-treble position, the toggle switch is flicked back and forth between the bridge and neck pickups, stopping at the middle pickup before moving into the next phrase.

The riff in measure 19 is one of the most devastating ever played by Hendrix (or anyone else). Though relatively simple in structure, it is difficult to pull off with the same *propulsion* Jimi generates. Part of the secret lies in the legato nature of two key spots: 1) the upbeat of beat 2 moving into the downbeat of beat 3, as a grace note B (second string, twelfth fret) is hammered up to D (fifteenth fret) and released back to B, followed by an A-to-B-to-A bend and release, a pull-off from A to G, and then an E (fourth string, fourteenth fret); 2) G-to-A hammer and instant A-to-B bend, followed by D (second string, fifteenth fret), A-to-B bend, and A-to-G pull-off, ending again on E. This entire phrase is delivered at lightning speed, with beautiful fluidity, precise clarity, and, as I say, *propulsion*. Be sure to study the slow version of this segment.

Fig. 42 **63** **64**

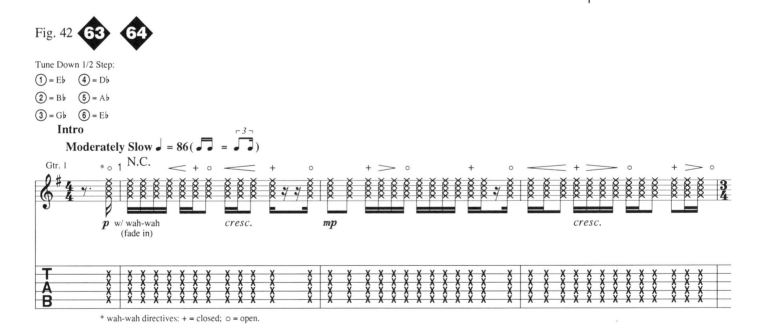

* wah-wah directives: + = closed; o = open.

Figure 43 – Verse and Chorus

During the first eight measures of the first verse, Jimi alternates between doubling his vocal phrases on guitar and playing "straight" rhythm. As is usually the case with Hendrix, there is *something* intricate happening on each sixteenth note of each beat in each measure, so exact duplication is quite difficult. Study every nuance; it's incredible what can be done with one E major chord and a couple of simple riffs. The single-note phrases are based on E minor pentatonic (E–G–A–B–D).

In measure 11, double-stops are used to allude to E7 (sometimes interpreted as G, as in Stevie Ray Vaughan's version of the tune). In measure 12, this shape shifts down (switching from a major sixth to a minor sixth) and functions as an A/C♯ chord. Measures 15 and 16 feature C9 and D7, respectively, followed by a return to similar E major chord figures. This segment is also performed slowly for closer study.

Figure 44 – Guitar Solo

This segment features the first sixteen measures of Jimi's classic solo on this tune. All of the improvisation is based on E minor pentatonic, and Hendrix clearly demonstrates just how much can be done with one little five-tone scale. Across the first four measures, a strong melody is presented, followed in measure 5 (actually beginning at the end of measure 4) with a slow-rising two-step bend recalling one of Jimi's heroes, Albert King.

The lick in measure 6 is a rhythmic nightmare; these licks were flying off the cuff, and the phrasing is a by-product of the overall effect of quickly alternating between B-to-D hammers and B-to-C♯ hammers. Don't just try to jam it all into the same space; listen to the slow version, and try to pick up on the internal logic of the phrase, however ambiguous it may seem to be.

Another barn burning riff is played in measures 9–12, as Jimi speeds up and slows down repeatedly, creating incredible tension and release. Once again, this is difficult to recreate with absolute rhythmic perfection, so don't make that a mandatory achievement; do your best to understand what Jimi is doing, and try to absorb the shape of the line, the articulation, and the delivery. Starting on beat 2 of measure 11, the wah is kicked on, and rocked quickly back and forth. Follow the wah directives closely to recreate this technique properly.

The segment ends with a return (not so "slight") to the E major chord patterns played earlier, again with some twists and turns.

Fig. 44 67 68

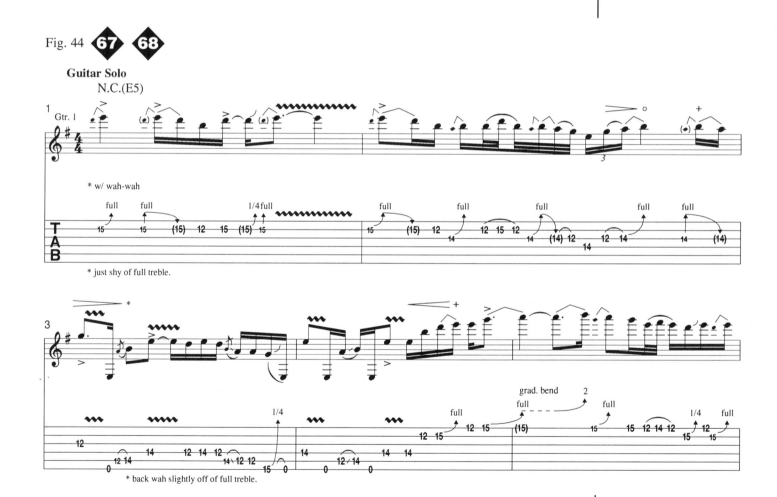

66

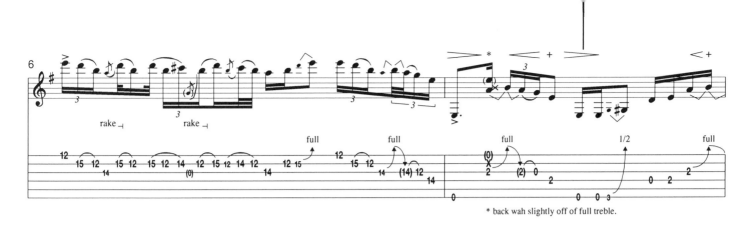

rake   rake

* back wah slightly off of full treble.

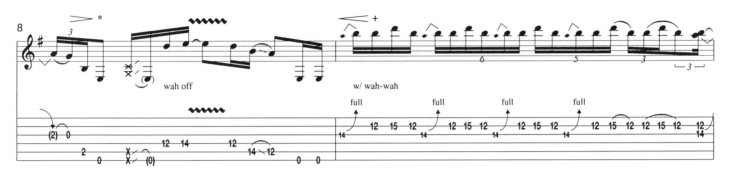

wah off   w/ wah-wah

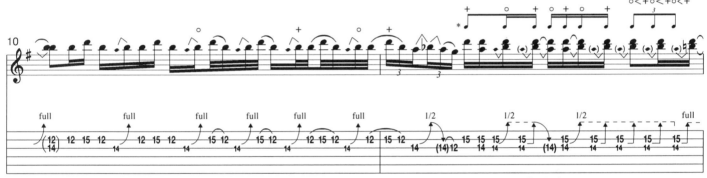

* Rock wah in specified rhythm.

(E)

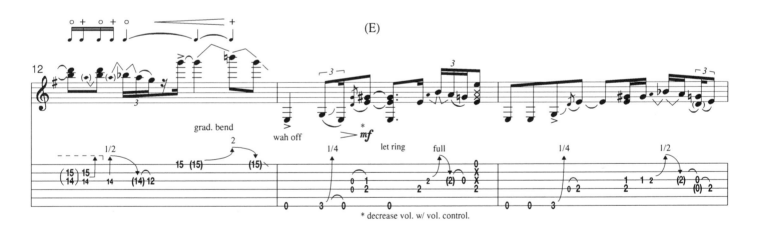

grad. bend   wah off   * mf   let ring

* decrease vol. w/ vol. control.

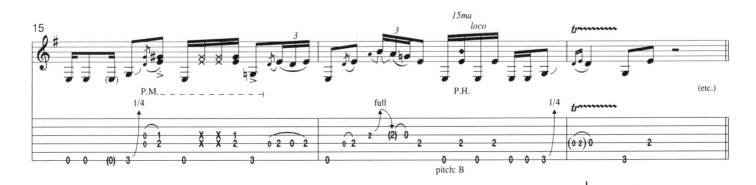

15ma
loco

P.M.   P.H.   (etc.)

pitch: B

BOLD AS LOVE

Words and Music by Jimi Hendrix

"Bold as Love" is as fine a representation of the genius of Jimi Hendrix as one could hope to find. Great ideas, execution, sound, spirit, attitude…and it's just a great, great *song*—pure, unadulterated Hendrix at its best.

Figure 45 – Introduction

After the powerful A major chord stab that aggressively kicks off this song, Jimi relies on the same chordal-fragment concept heard on other tunes such as "Little Wing," "Castles Made of Sand," and "The Wind Cries Mary." Like "Voodoo Child (Slight Return)," every square inch of each measure is filled with improvisation, so slow, careful study is a must. There are many examples of "oblique motion" (one note remains stationary while the other changes), as in measures 1 and 6, as well as of chordal arpeggiations (chords played in a fragmented fashion, one-note-at-a-time), heard in measures 6 and 8. In measure 8, a second guitar enters, which supplies double-stop sixths played in alternating sixteenth-note sextuplets. Gtr. 1, the primary rhythm guitar, is heard in the right channel, and Gtr. 2, the secondary guitar, is heard in the left channel.

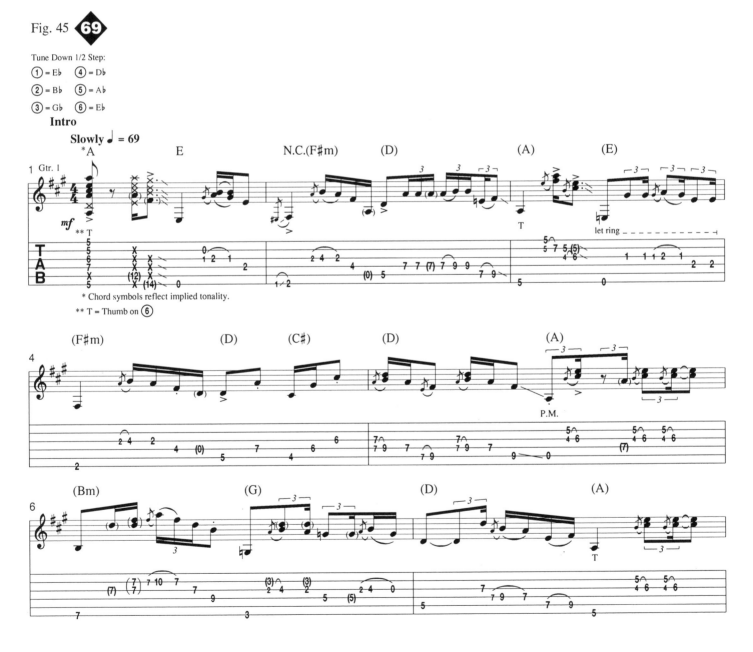

Fig. 45

Copyright © 1968, 1977, 1980 by EXPERIENCE HENDRIX, L.L.C.
Copyright Renewed 1996
All Rights Controlled and Administered by EXPERIENCE HENDRIX, L.L.C.
All Rights Reserved

(etc.)

(etc.)

Figure 46 – Chorus

Again, the guitars are split left and right, with the primary guitar (Gtr. 1) laying down chord voicings on the top three strings, and the secondary guitar (Gtr. 2) continuing to add double-stops in sixths. In measures 2 and 3, Gtr. 2 switches from sixteenth-note sextuplets to tremolo picking (which means to strum the double-stops as fast as possible).

In the primary rhythm guitar part, notice how the pinky is used to hammer on and pull off notes on the high E string in measures 2 and 4.

Fig. 46 **70**

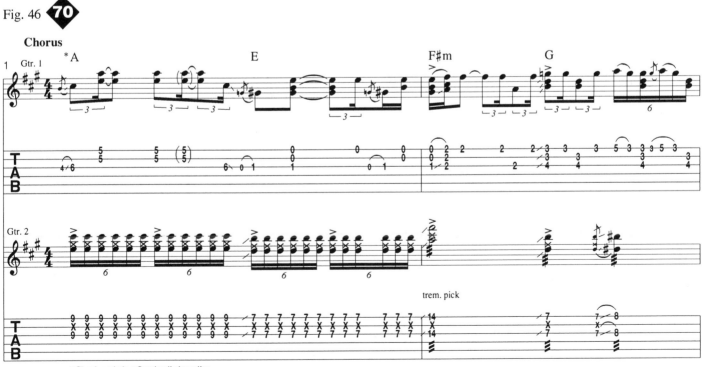

*Chord symbols reflect implied tonality.

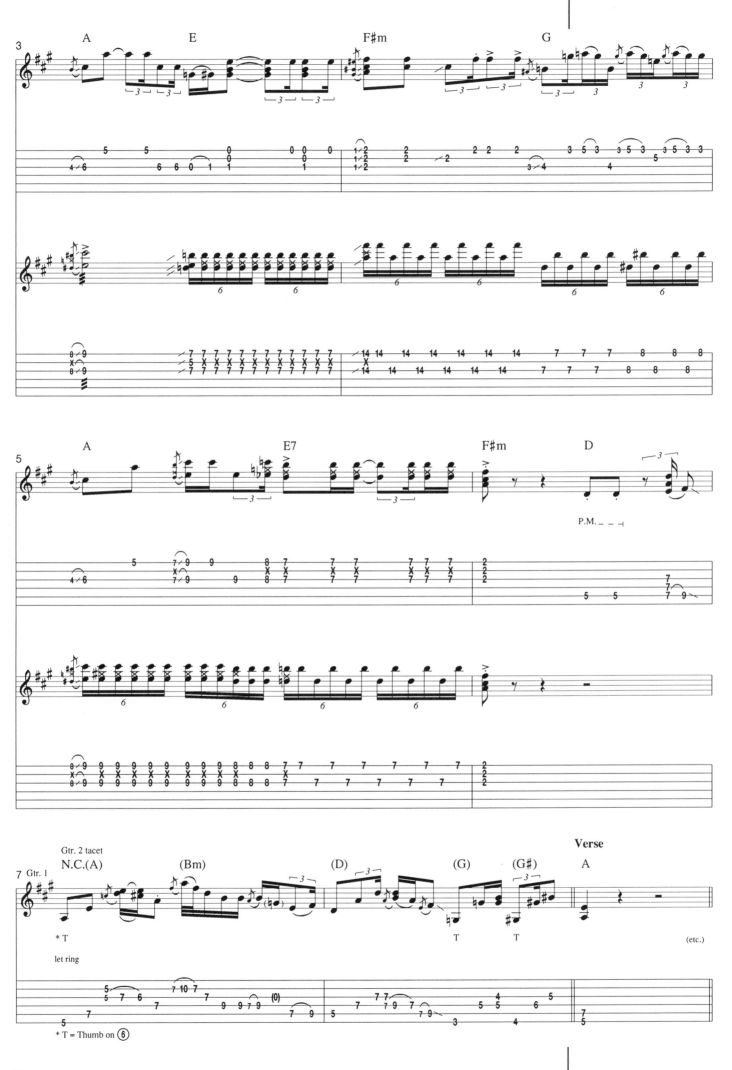

Figure 47 – Guitar Solo

Well, what can you say? This is simply one of the greatest guitar solos ever played in the entire history of recorded music. First, the rhythm part: the chord progression behind the solo is essentially the same as the first two measures of the verse progression, except the last chord of the verse progression, D, is switched for G; the resulting progression is A–E–F♯m–G. This two-measure figure is played six and a half times and culminates with the F♯m in a 2/4 measure, followed by a repeated D-to-A chord pattern and ending with a held A5 power chord.

Jimi's timeless solo is slow and melodic, and moves between A minor pentatonic (A–C–D–E–G) and A major pentatonic (A–B–C♯–E–F♯). A major pentatonic relates well to the F♯m chord, because the notes of A major pentatonic also comprise F♯ minor pentatonic (F♯–A–B–C♯–E)—the two scales just start at a different points in the series. This is because A is the "relative major" of F♯ minor. The solo begins with A minor pentatonic (measure 2) but immediately moves to A major pentatonic (the ♭7th, G, appears abundantly), and stays there for measures 3–6. Measure 7 reverts to A minor pentatonic, switching back to A major pentatonic (with the inclusion of D and G, making reference to A Mixolydian—A–B–C♯–D–E–F♯–G) for measures 8–16. Jimi ends the solo (measures 17–19) with A minor pentatonic licks. And the tone? Killer!

Fig. 47

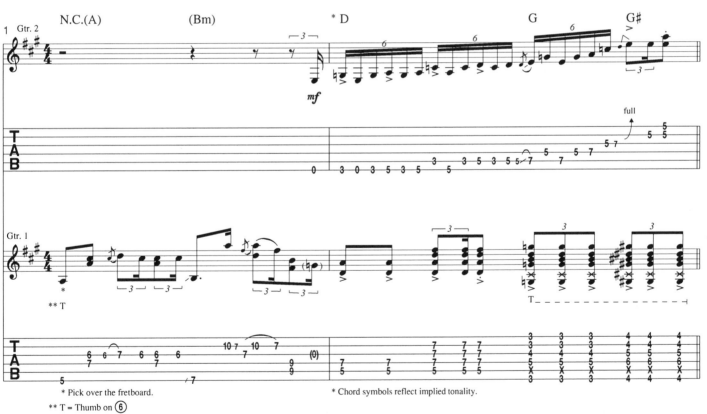

* Pick over the fretboard. * Chord symbols reflect implied tonality.

** T = Thumb on ⑥

Guitar Solo

* Turn on Fuzz Face immediately after picking first note.

* Pick w/ edge of thumb.

* slight vibrato

Figure 48 – Outro-Guitar Solo

Hendrix provided a fantastic twist—a *vertical lift*—to this tune by modulating up two whole steps, to C♯, for the outro. The chord progression (played by Jimi on harpsichord) is the same as before but transposed to C♯: C♯–G♯–A♯m–B. The segment, as recorded here, is presented with guitar, bass, and drums only, for easier examination of the guitar solo.

In the first two measures of this solo, Jimi quotes the opening of the first solo. (Compare the two to see how close they really are, melodically and rhythmically.) In measures 2–5, Jimi plays unison bends nearly exclusively. In measures 6–11, the improvisation is based on C♯ major pentatonic (C♯–D♯–E♯–G♯–A♯) with a couple bits of weirdness. In measure 7, it sounds like Jimi makes a mistake, fretting a G instead of G♯. To compensate, he bends the G up one whole step, but this isn't enough—A is still outside the scale. On the downbeat of measure 8, beat 1, he bends the note again—this time bending it 1 1/2 steps to A♯ and then releases the bend one step, to G♯. This kind-of-funky, not-perfectly-in-tune approach gives personality to the solo. Doing something "right" is not always "best"; the ability to turn a potential disaster into a moment of glory is a quality possessed by all the greats.

In measures 12–15, Jimi plays a pull-off lick that moves through each chord in the progression, essentially arpeggiating each chord. C♯ is outlined with the notes of a C♯ major triad (C♯–E♯–G♯), G♯ is outlined with the notes of a G♯ major triad (G♯–B♯–D♯), A♯m is outlined with the notes of a A♯ minor triad (A♯–C♯–E♯), and B is outlined with the notes of a B major triad (B–D♯–F♯). Jimi throws in a little chromaticism, inserting a C major triad (C–E–G), played as pull-offs, between B and C♯.

In measures 16 and 17, Jimi reverts back to minor pentatonic, here in the key of C♯ (C♯–E–F♯–G♯–B). These hard-driving lines are peaked with the furiously repeated two-step bends in measure 18. Measure 19 features the use of the C♯ blues scale (C♯–E–F♯–G–G♯–B), and in measure 20, Jimi repeatedly bends the root note (C♯, fourth string, eleventh fret), followed by a dip into C♯ major pentatonic in measure 21. Measures 22 and 23 utilize C♯ minor pentatonic, and Jimi rounds off this beautiful solo with thirty-second-note (and tremolo-picked) double-stops, which relate directly to the chords they are played over. The entire track is treated with a Leslie/rotating speaker effect.

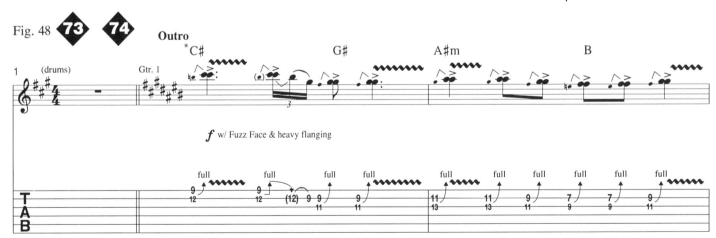

* Chord symbols reflect implied tonality.

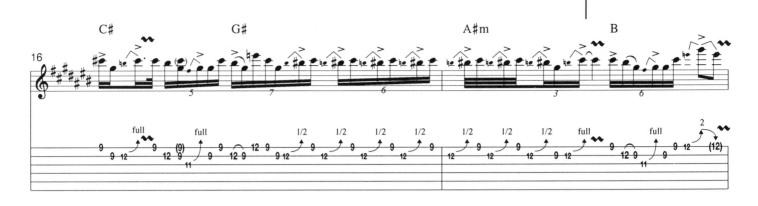

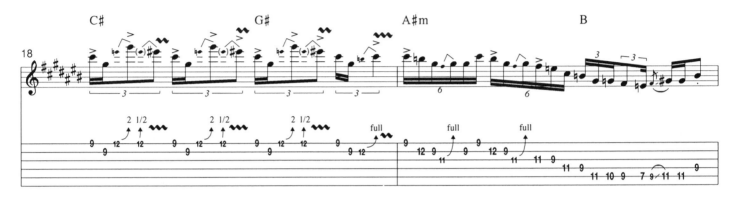

Begin Fade

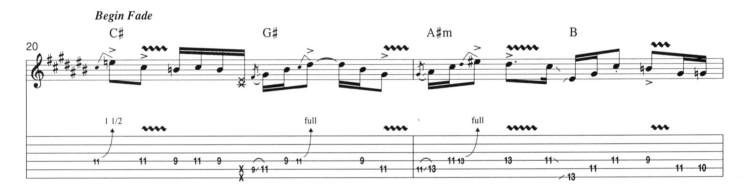

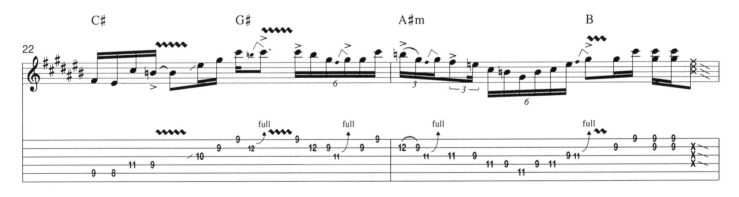

Fade Out

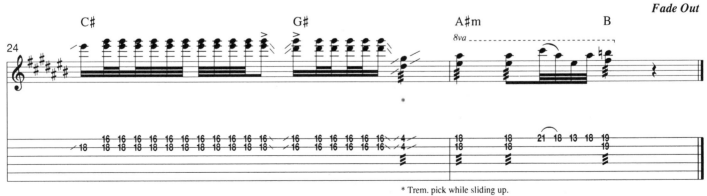

* Trem. pick while sliding up.

Guitar Notation Legend

Guitar Music can be notated three different ways: on a *musical staff*, in *tablature*, and in *rhythm slashes*.

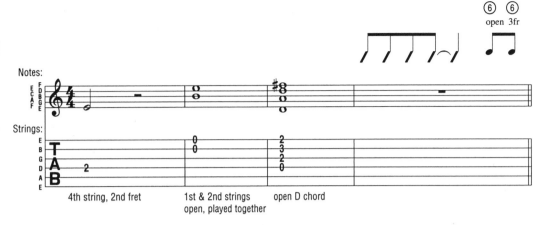

RHYTHM SLASHES are written above the staff. Strum chords in the rhythm indicated. Use the chord diagrams found at the top of the first page of the transcription for the appropriate chord voicings. Round noteheads indicate single notes.

THE MUSICAL STAFF shows pitches and rhythms and is divided by bar lines into measures. Pitches are named after the first seven letters of the alphabet.

TABLATURE graphically represents the guitar fingerboard. Each horizontal line represents a a string, and each number represents a fret.

4th string, 2nd fret

1st & 2nd strings open, played together

open D chord

Definitions for Special Guitar Notation

HALF-STEP BEND: Strike the note and bend up 1/2 step.

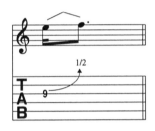

WHOLE-STEP BEND: Strike the note and bend up one step.

GRACE NOTE BEND: Strike the note and bend up as indicated. The first note does not take up any time.

SLIGHT (MICROTONE) BEND: Strike the note and bend up 1/4 step.

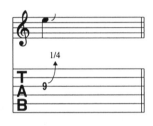

BEND AND RELEASE: Strike the note and bend up as indicated, then release back to the original note. Only the first note is struck.

PRE-BEND: Bend the note as indicated, then strike it.

PRE-BEND AND RELEASE: Bend the note as indicated. Strike it and release the bend back to the original note.

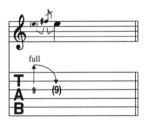

UNISON BEND: Strike the two notes simultaneously and bend the lower note up to the pitch of the higher.

VIBRATO: The string is vibrated by rapidly bending and releasing the note with the fretting hand.

WIDE VIBRATO: The pitch is varied to a greater degree by vibrating with the fretting hand.

HAMMER-ON: Strike the first (lower) note with one finger, then sound the higher note (on the same string) with another finger by fretting it without picking.

PULL-OFF: Place both fingers on the notes to be sounded. Strike the first note and without picking, pull the finger off to sound the second (lower) note.

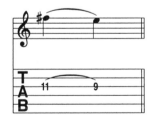

LEGATO SLIDE: Strike the first note and then slide the same fret-hand finger up or down to the second note. The second note is not struck.

SHIFT SLIDE: Same as legato slide, except the second note is struck.

TRILL: Very rapidly alternate between the notes indicated by continuously hammering on and pulling off.

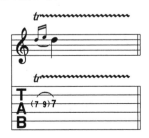

TAPPING: Hammer ("tap") the fret indicated with the pick-hand index or middle finger and pull off to the note fretted by the fret hand.

NATURAL HARMONIC: Strike the note while the fret-hand lightly touches the string directly over the fret indicated.

Harm.

PINCH HARMONIC: The note is fretted normally and a harmonic is produced by adding the edge of the thumb or the tip of the index finger of the pick hand to the normal pick attack.

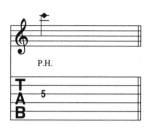

P.H.

HARP HARMONIC: The note is fretted normally and a harmonic is produced by gently resting the pick hand's index finger directly above the indicated fret (in parentheses) while the pick hand's thumb or pick assists by plucking the appropriate string.

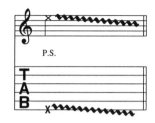

8va

H.H.

PICK SCRAPE: The edge of the pick is rubbed down (or up) the string, producing a scratchy sound.

P.S.

MUFFLED STRINGS: A percussive sound is produced by laying the fret hand across the string(s) without depressing, and striking them with the pick hand.

PALM MUTING: The note is partially muted by the pick hand lightly touching the string(s) just before the bridge.

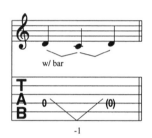

P.M.

RAKE: Drag the pick across the strings indicated with a single motion.

rake

TREMOLO PICKING: The note is picked as rapidly and continuously as possible.

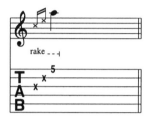

ARPEGGIATE: Play the notes of the chord indicated by quickly rolling them from bottom to top.

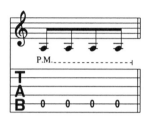

VIBRATO BAR DIVE AND RETURN: The pitch of the note or chord is dropped a specified number of steps (in rhythm) then returned to the original pitch.

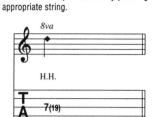

w/ bar

-1

VIBRATO BAR SCOOP: Depress the bar just before striking the note, then quickly release the bar.

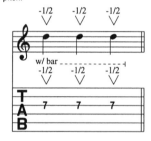

w/ bar

VIBRATO BAR DIP: Strike the note and then immediately drop a specified number of steps, then release back to the original pitch.

w/ bar

Additional Musical Definitions

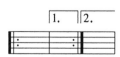	*(accent)*	• Accentuate note (play it louder)
	(accent)	• Accentuate note with great intensity
	(staccato)	• Play the note short
		• Downstroke
∨		• Upstroke

D.S. al Coda — • Go back to the sign (𝄋), then play until the measure marked "*To Coda*," then skip to the section labelled "*Coda*."

D.S. al Fine — • Go back to the beginning of the song and play until the measure marked "*Fine*" (end).

Rhy. Fig. — • Label used to recall a recurring accompaniment pattern (usually chordal).

Riff — • Label used to recall composed, melodic lines (usually single notes) which recur.

Fill — • Label used to identify a brief melodic figure which is to be inserted into the arrangement.

Rhy. Fill — • A chordal version of a Fill.

tacet — • Instrument is silent (drops out).

• Repeat measures between signs.

1. 2. — • When a repeated section has different endings, play the first ending only the first time and the second ending only the second time.

NOTE: Tablature numbers in parentheses mean:
1. The note is being sustained over a system (note in standard notation is tied), or
2. The note is sustained, but a new articulation (such as a hammer-on, pull-off, slide or vibrato begins, or
3. The note is a barely audible "ghost" note (note in standard notation is also in parentheses).

GUITAR *signature licks*

Signature Licks book/CD packs provide a step-by-step breakdown of "right from the record" riffs, licks, and solos so you can jam along with your favorite bands. They contain performance notes and an overview of each artist's or group's style, with note-for-note transcriptions in notes and tab. The CDs feature full-band demos at both normal and slow speeds.

BEST OF ACOUSTIC GUITAR
00695640 ....$19.95

AEROSMITH 1973-1979
00695106 ....$22.95

AEROSMITH 1979-1998
00695219 ....$22.95

BEST OF AGGRO-METAL
00695592 ....$19.95

BEST OF CHET ATKINS
00695752 ....$22.95

THE BEACH BOYS DEFINITIVE COLLECTION
00695683 ....$22.95

BEST OF THE BEATLES FOR ACOUSTIC GUITAR
00695453 ....$22.95

THE BEATLES BASS
00695283 ....$22.95

THE BEATLES FAVORITES
00695096 ....$24.95

THE BEATLES HITS
00695049 ....$24.95

BEST OF GEORGE BENSON
00695418 ....$22.95

BEST OF BLACK SABBATH
00695249 ....$22.95

BEST OF BLINK - 182
00695704 ....$22.95

BEST OF BLUES GUITAR
00695846 ....$19.95

BLUES GUITAR CLASSICS
00695177 ....$19.95

BLUES/ROCK GUITAR MASTERS
00695348 ....$19.95

BEST OF CHARLIE CHRISTIAN
00695584 ....$22.95

BEST OF ERIC CLAPTON
00695038 ....$24.95

ERIC CLAPTON – THE BLUESMAN
00695040 ....$22.95

ERIC CLAPTON – FROM THE ALBUM UNPLUGGED
00695250 ....$24.95

BEST OF CREAM
00695251 ....$22.95

DEEP PURPLE – GREATEST HITS
00695625 ....$22.95

THE BEST OF DEF LEPPARD
00696516 ....$22.95

THE DOORS
00695373 ....$22.95

FAMOUS ROCK GUITAR SOLOS
00695590 ....$19.95

BEST OF FOO FIGHTERS
00695481 ....$22.95

GREATEST GUITAR SOLOS OF ALL TIME
00695301 ....$19.95

BEST OF GRANT GREEN
00695747 ....$22.95

GUITAR INSTRUMENTAL HITS
00695309 ....$19.95

GUITAR RIFFS OF THE '60S
00695218 ....$19.95

BEST OF GUNS N' ROSES
00695183 ....$22.95

HARD ROCK SOLOS
00695591 ....$19.95

JIMI HENDRIX
00696560 ....$24.95

HOT COUNTRY GUITAR
00695580 ....$19.95

BEST OF JAZZ GUITAR
00695586 ....$24.95

ERIC JOHNSON
00699317 ....$22.95

ROBERT JOHNSON
00695264 ....$22.95

THE ESSENTIAL ALBERT KING
00695713 ....$22.95

B.B. KING – THE DEFINITIVE COLLECTION
00695635 ....$22.95

THE KINKS
00695553 ....$22.95

BEST OF KISS
00699413 ....$22.95

MARK KNOPFLER
00695178 ....$22.95

BEST OF YNGWIE MALMSTEEN
00695669 ....$22.95

BEST OF PAT MARTINO
00695632 ....$22.95

MEGADETH
00695041 ....$22.95

WES MONTGOMERY
00695387 ....$22.95

BEST OF NIRVANA
00695483 ....$24.95

THE OFFSPRING
00695852 ....$24.95

VERY BEST OF OZZY OSBOURNE
00695431 ....$22.95

BEST OF JOE PASS
00695730 ....$22.95

PINK FLOYD – EARLY CLASSICS
00695566 ....$22.95

THE POLICE
00695724 ....$22.95

THE GUITARS OF ELVIS
00696507 ....$22.95

BEST OF QUEEN
00695097 ....$22.95

BEST OF RAGE AGAINST THE MACHINE
00695480 ....$22.95

RED HOT CHILI PEPPERS
00695173 ....$22.95

RED HOT CHILI PEPPERS – GREATEST HITS
00695828 ....$24.95

BEST OF DJANGO REINHARDT
00695660 ....$22.95

BEST OF ROCK
00695884 ....$19.95

BEST OF ROCK 'N' ROLL GUITAR
00695559 ....$19.95

BEST OF ROCKABILLY GUITAR
00695785 ....$19.95

THE ROLLING STONES
00695079 ....$22.95

BEST OF JOE SATRIANI
00695216 ....$22.95

BEST OF SILVERCHAIR
00695488 ....$22.95

THE BEST OF SOUL GUITAR
00695703 ....$19.95

BEST OF SOUTHERN ROCK
00695703 ....$19.95

ROD STEWART
00695663 ....$22.95

BEST OF SYSTEM OF A DOWN
00695788 ....$22.95

STEVE VAI
00673247 ....$22.95

STEVE VAI – ALIEN LOVE SECRETS: THE NAKED VAMPS
00695223 ....$22.95

STEVE VAI – FIRE GARDEN: THE NAKED VAMPS
00695166 ....$22.95

STEVE VAI – THE ULTRA ZONE: NAKED VAMPS
00695684 ....$22.95

STEVIE RAY VAUGHAN
00699316 ....$24.95

THE GUITAR STYLE OF STEVIE RAY VAUGHAN
00695155 ....$24.95

BEST OF THE VENTURES
00695772 ....$19.95

THE WHO
00695561 ....$22.95

BEST OF ZZ TOP
00695738 ....$22.95

Complete descriptions and songlists online!

FOR MORE INFORMATION, SEE YOUR LOCAL MUSIC DEALER, OR WRITE TO:

HAL•LEONARD® CORPORATION
7777 W. BLUEMOUND RD. P.O. BOX 13819 MILWAUKEE, WI 53213

www.halleonard.com
Prices, contents and availability subject to change without notice.

0606

Hendrix Publications from Hal Leonard

Jimi Hendrix – The Lyrics
Compiled by Janie Hendrix

This book includes numerous examples of Jimi's handwritten lyrics and photos of Jimi accompanying every song. Songs include: Purple Haze • Foxey Lady • Voodoo Chile • The Wind Cries Mary • Dolly Dagger • Are You Experienced? • and more.

00330982 ....$27.00

Are You Experienced

11 songs: Are You Experienced • Foxey Lady • Hey Joe • Manic Depression • Purple Haze • The Wind Cries Mary • and more.

00692930	Guitar Recorded Versions	$24.95
00660097	Easy Recorded Versions	$12.95
00690371	Bass Recorded Versions	$16.95
00690372	Drum Recorded Versions	$14.95
00672308	Transcribed Scores (17 songs)	$29.95

Axis: Bold as Love

13 songs: Bold as Love • Castles Made of Sand • Little Wing • Spanish Castle Magic • and more.

00692931	Guitar Recorded Versions	$22.95
00690373	Bass Recorded Versions	$14.95
00672345	Transcribed Scores	$29.95

Band of Gypsys

Contains note-for-note transcriptions of: Who Knows • Machine Gun • Changes • Power to Love • Message of Love • We Gotta Live Together. Includes introduction and playing tips.

00690304	Guitar Recorded Versions	$22.95
00672313	Transcribed Scores	$29.95

Highlights from the BBC Sessions

Guitar transcriptions of 15 tunes from Hendrix's live BBC broadcasts: Day Tripper • Hey Joe • Hound Dog • I Was Made to Love Her • I'm Your Hoochie Coochie Man • Sunshine of Your Love • and more.

00690321 Guitar Recorded Versions $22.95

Blues

10 transcriptions of Jimi's most popular blues tunes complete with an extensive introduction and photo section: Born Under a Bad Sign • Catfish Blues • Hear My Train a Comin' • Once I Had a Woman • Red House • Voodoo Chile Blues • and more.

00694944 Guitar Recorded Versions.....................$24.95

Electric Ladyland

16 songs: All Along the Watchtower • Have You Ever Been (To Electric Ladyland) • Voodoo Child (Slight Return) • and more.

00692932	Guitar Recorded Versions	$24.95
00672311	Transcribed Scores	$29.95

Radio One

All 17 songs on the album in authoritative transcriptions with detailed players' notes and photographs. Songs: Hear My Train a Comin' • Hound Dog • Fire • Purple Haze • Hey Joe • Foxey Lady • and more.

00660099 Guitar Recorded Versions $24.95

Smash Hits

Hendrix's 1969 best-of compilation of 12 songs: All Along the Watchtower • Crosstown Traffic • Fire • Foxey Lady • Hey Joe • Purple Haze • Remember • Stone Free • The Wind Cries Mary.

00690602	Guitar Recorded Versions	$19.95
00699223	Guitar Play-Along	$17.95
00699835	Drum Play-Along	$16.95

Wild Blue Angel

All 18 songs from *Jimi Hendrix – Live at the Isle of Wight*. Includes: All Along the Watchtower • Dolly Dagger • Foxey Lady • Freedom • Machine Gun • Sgt. Pepper's Lonely Hearts Club Band • and more.

00690608 Guitar Recorded Versions $24.95

Woodstock

Relive Hendrix's Woodstock performance with these 11 songs: Red House • Star Spangled Banner • Villanova Junction • and more. Includes photos.

00690017 Guitar Recorded Versions $24.95

Experience Hendrix – Book One Beginning Guitar Method
by Michael Johnson

This step-by-step process of learning music using the songs of Jimi Hendrix teaches guitar basics, music basics, music/guitar theory, scales, chords, reading music, guidelines for practicing, tips on caring for your guitar, and much more.

00695159 Book/CD Pack.......................................$14.95

Jimi Hendrix – Experience Hendrix

20 of Hendrix's best: All Along the Watchtower • Bold as Love • Castles Made of Sand • Foxey Lady • Hey Joe • Manic Depression • Purple Haze • Star Spangled Banner • The Wind Cries Mary • and more.

00672397 Transcribed Scores.............................$29.95

In Deep with Jimi Hendrix
by Andy Aledort

This book breaks down and reassembles the solos, riffs, rhythm figures, harmony lines, ensemble parts, and more from over 40 of Hendrix' greatest songs.

00660335 Guitar School $19.95

Jimi Hendrix Anthology

73 songs from all of his recordings: Are You Experienced? • Freedom • Gypsy Eyes • Hear My Train a Comin' • I Don't Live Today • My Friend • Stepping Stone • and more. Includes photos.

00306930 Melody/Lyrics/Chords...........................$22.50

Jimi Hendrix – Signature Licks
by Andy Aledort

Performance notes, chord voicings, scale use, and unusual techniques are included for 12 songs: Foxey Lady • Hey Joe • Little Wing • Purple Haze • and more.

00696560 Book/CD Pack.....................................$24.95

Jimi Hendrix – Learn to Play the Songs from *Are You Experienced*

This DVD shows guitarists how to play parts of every song on this album. Songs: Purple Haze • Love or Confusion • The Wind Cries Mary • Fire • Third Stone from the Sun • Can You See Me • and more.

00320274 DVD $59.95

Study the master with these transcriptions and explorations of the techniques and tunes that made Hendrix a legend.

Prices, contents, and availability subject to change without notice.

0807